INTER-REPUBLICAN COOPERATION OF THE
RUSSIAN REPUBLIC

This book was first written as the author's Ph.D dissertation and submitted to the Graduate College of The University of Arizona, Tucson, Arizona, USA, in 1995.

To my brother,
Farid Ahmed Bhuiyan

Inter-Republican Cooperation of the Russian Republic

ANWARA BEGUM
Chittagong University
Chittagong, Bangladesh

LONDON AND NEW YORK

First published 1997 by Ashgate Publishing

Reissued 2018 by Routledge
2 Park Square, Milton Park, Abingdon, Oxon OX14 4RN
711 Third Avenue, New York, NY 10017, USA

Routledge is an imprint of the Taylor & Francis Group, an informa business

Copyright © Anwara Begum 1997

All rights reserved. No part of this book may be reprinted or reproduced or utilised in any form or by any electronic, mechanical, or other means, now known or hereafter invented, including photocopying and recording, or in any information storage or retrieval system, without permission in writing from the publishers.

Notice:
Product or corporate names may be trademarks or registered trademarks, and are used only for identification and explanation without intent to infringe.

Publisher's Note
The publisher has gone to great lengths to ensure the quality of this reprint but points out that some imperfections in the original copies may be apparent.

Disclaimer
The publisher has made every effort to trace copyright holders and welcomes correspondence from those they have been unable to contact.

ISBN 13: 978-1-138-31567-9 (hbk)
ISBN 13: 978-1-138-31568-6 (pbk)
ISBN 13: 978-0-429-45619-0 (ebk)

Contents

List of Tables		*vii*
1	Introduction and Literature Review	1
2	Theoretical Orientation and Research Design	9
3	The Flow of Interactions: The Nature of Transactions between Russia and its Partners	27
4	Reciprocity in Unequal Relations: A Case Study of Lithuanian-Russian Cooperation	43
5	Lithuania Plays the Russia Card: Lithuanian-Russian Relations and the USSR	63
6	Through the Eyes of the Russian Government: Content Analysis of Elite Pronouncements	82
7	Russian Treaties: The Interplay of Multilateral and Bilateral Relations	104
8	Conclusion	125

vi *Inter-republican cooperation*

Appendix A   *139*
Appendix B   *142*
Appendix C   *143*
Appendix D   *145*

Bibliography   *147*

Index   *156*

List of Tables

3.1	Russia's cooperation with other republics (June 1990-August 1991)	29
3.2	Cooperation in 1990 and 1991	30
6.1	Themes appearing in Russian elites' statements	89
6.2	Themes uttered in 1990 and 1991	90
6.3	Distribution of themes by republics	91
6.4	Distribution of themes by republics	92
6.5	Distribution of themes by republics	93

1 Introduction and Literature Review

Introduction

The Chechen crisis which began in early December 1994 prompted such reformers as Egor Gaider and Grigori Yavlinsky to distance themselves from the Yeltsin government. The Russian media portrayed Yeltsin as closeted with his Soviet era advisors and associates. Such isolation of Yeltsin from the reformist democratic forces was perceived by many as somehow a more recent development and his government's aggressive posturing towards the near abroad as an ominous new phenomenon. Some Russian observers even called Russia's behaviour towards the newly independent countries 'frivolous.' The image of Yeltsin as the 'new authoritarian' or Yeltsin the 'helpless, isolated Tsar' manipulated by officials from the Communist elite of the Soviet Union was the result of our relative ignorance of the Russian state and its burgeoning elite's behaviour in the period when Russia was trying to define itself as a separate state.

Russia's politics in the late Soviet period when it was separating itself from the central authority of the Soviet Union has been somewhat neglected. That is why its behaviour in many instances appears to be new development and the character of its government surprises us. One of the many aspects of Russian politics that has not received adequate attention is a process of inter-republican cooperation that the new Russian government conducted in the period 1990-1991.

The year 1990 saw two rival political processes unfold in the Soviet Union both of which aimed at the reconfiguration of an aspect of the Soviet

2 Inter-republican cooperation

state structure. One of them, the Union Treaty process, was initiated by the Soviet President, Mikhail Gorbachev, and had the goal to renew the Soviet state as a federation. The other, inter-republican cooperation of the Russian Federation government under Boris Yeltsin's leadership was to culminate in the recognition of the republics of the Soviet Union as independent states. It is probably due to our lingering bias for formal institutions and their interactions that we devoted more attention to the unsuccessful attempt of the USSR President than the ultimately successful strategy of Russia -- a republic that was emerging as a separate state.

Inter-republican cooperation can be defined as, but was not limited to, signing treaties promoting economic and technical cooperation, bestowing symbolic importance through head of the state level visits, and verbally supporting another republic's struggle for independence. Russia became engaged in such activities immediately after the formation of the Russian government in June 1990. Even before the government was formed, Yeltsin, after his election to the Russian Congress of People's Deputies, expressed the desire to develop relations with the rest of the republics on the basis of treaties. Although it was the other republics, specifically the Baltic ones, which initiated inter-republican cooperation, Russia came to dominate the process.

Nothing has been written on the inter-republican cooperation of the Russian Republic.[1] As a matter of fact, the politics of the Russian Soviet Federated Socialist Republic (RSFSR) when it was trying to separate itself from the centre has been somewhat neglected. Very little has been written on cooperation among all the republics in general in the late Gorbachev period. The few studies that have considered such cooperation in some form -- brief remarks, short discussion or exclusive focus -- incorporate Russian cooperation in the broad concept of inter-republican cooperation.

In the chapters that follow I study the RSFSR's cooperation with the rest of the Soviet republics combining a number of research methods and situating the whole study in the theories developed in comparative politics. It is true that other republics were establishing cooperative relations with one another, but Russia's cooperation presents some important and interesting research questions.

Russia was not just another republic trying to gain independence from the centre but itself was the centre. A Russian dominated Communist Party was governing the Soviet Union. It was not an instance of manoeuvring in a nationalist struggle like any other republic. Russia's cooperative posture looked very much like the effort of a sub-national elite hostile to the Communist elite to reorganize Russia's relations with the republics. Also, it resembled the effort by a more flexible elite to manage the break-up of an empire so the ruling ethnic group, in this case the Russians, would not lose much. The questions this phenomenon generates are: 1. Was the cooperation an effort to undermine the governing elite of a state by a rival elite governing a sub-national administrative unit which had earlier broke away from the governing elite? 2. Was the cooperation also an attempt by the more liberal rival elite to salvage as much as possible out of an empire that could not be retained in the old form? 3. If the answers to both 1 and 2 are yes, then how can elite conflict -- a concern in elite theory -- influence the way the break-up of an empire is managed -- a concern in theories of empires? These are the overarching issues addressed in this study.

In an attempt to analyse Russia's cooperative strategy, I ask why the Russian Republic engaged in cooperative actions, actions that were supportive of other republics (more detailed definition of cooperation given later). Was it economic necessity as one author suggests (Seliverstov, 1991) and another seems to think (Bahry, 1991) or were there other reasons? The book is an attempt to find out whether two propositions can be supported with evidence. The propositions are: 1. The Russian Republic cooperated with the other republics to render the central government irrelevant. 2. It cooperated to manage the breakdown of the Soviet state occurring at the time. The first proposition addresses the first question stated in the paragraph above; the second one relates to the second issue. The findings of the research will address the third question.

Features of inter-republican cooperation

Inter-republican cooperation started as a process of general cooperation among republics. It had two phases. Cooperation among unofficial groups on the one hand and among individuals on the other marked the first phase; cooperation among republican governments defined the second phase.

In the first phase, some informal groups declared their support of, or solidarity with, another group in a different republic, as the *Moscow Popular Front* did for the *Lithuanian Popular Front* (Kagarlitsky, 1990). The formation of some groups was taking place in republics other than the home republics of the groups. One example of this is the founding Congress of the *Belarusian Popular Front* in Vilnius, Lithuania, not in Minsk, Belarus. Residents of one republic participated in demonstrations in another republic; for example Armenians demonstrating in Lithuania (Butterfield, 1990; Senn, 1990).

The first phase also saw some groups promoting inter-republican cooperation come into existence. The *Inter-regional Group of Peoples'*

4 Inter-republican cooperation

Deputies was the most important and visible of such groups. Excepting the Turkmen republic, all the republics were represented in the group by at least one representative. There was the *Centre of Peoples Enslaved by the Soviet Union*; the radical democratic movements of Estonia, Armenia, Georgia, Lithuania, Latvia, Tataria, Ukraine, and Belarus participated in it.[2]

In the second phase, the republican governments were interacting with one another. It is the second phase in the case of Russia on which this study focuses. This phase started with the Baltic republics initiating economic cooperation among themselves.[3] Then, against the backdrop of the central government's economic blockade of Lithuania, the Moscow City Soviet decided to send aid to Lithuania, and Boris Yeltsin, the then Chairman of the Russian Federation Supreme Soviet, promised to send supplies to Lithuania. Soon the Central Asian republics joined the process. Later, different republican governments were signing statements, treaties of economic cooperation, and treaties of general cooperation; authoritative government figures were making statements that republics would support one another against threats to their sovereignty, as did Boris Yeltsin.[4]

Toward the end of 1990, the Soviet republics, in an intensified regional cooperation process, were signing all kinds of agreements among themselves. Examples of such agreements would be the broad cooperation treaty signed by Belarus and Ukraine at the end of 1990 and the trade agreement signed by Ukraine and Estonia in early 1991. The Russian Republic was a prominent actor in this process of inter-republican cooperative activities.

Inter-republican cooperation can be understood as supporting another republic in its quest for independence and apprehension of punitive measures used by the Union government in Moscow. In addition, signing economic, social, and cultural agreements with other republics formed a part of such cooperation. It appeared as a significant political process at the end of the Gorbachev period. The Russian Republic, like the other two large republics, i.e., Kazakhstan and Ukraine, became involved in this inter-republican politics, as it seemed then, like a naturally important actor.

Inter-republican cooperation has not been one of the grand events like the weakening of the Communist Party of the Soviet Union, the breakup of the Soviet Union, or the formation of the new *Commonwealth of Independent States*; consequently, it has yet to receive adequate attention from researchers. The same is true of Russia's cooperation. Russia and the Russians were the dominant elements in the Soviet scheme of governance. The fact that they suddenly started identifying with the separatist nationalism of the republics in itself should be one of the most intriguing enigmas to be explored. There have been scattered references to and discussions of inter-republican cooperation which of course incorporate Russia's cooperation as well.

Literature review

Two sets of writings are available on the two phases of inter-republican cooperation. The first deals with non-governmental cooperation and is not relevant to this study since this is a study of government level cooperation.[5] The second set of writings deals with inter-republican cooperation at the government level. Like the first set this one also does not focus on the Russian Republic but includes it by implication. Two perspectives have been offered by it -- economic (Bahry and Seliverstov) and political (Motyl and Willerton), both views presenting Russia as the same kind of actor -- one of the fifteen republics.

The economic perspective itself incorporates two different views on the phenomenon. One of them depicts it as a concerted effort to sustain the preexisting economic ties with the other republics (Bahry, 1991). Many of the inter-republican agreements were attempts by the republics at sustaining the existing economic ties among them which were being disrupted by the reform process. The other view presents it as a nascent process of regional integration (Seliverstov, 1991). The inter-republican interaction system that existed before the initiation of Gorbachev's reform was a centrally controlled process and had many irrationalities inherent in it. The Gorbachev administration did not pay much attention to the regional interactions at the beginning, but started showing concern much later. The republics themselves began signing economic cooperation treaties. This -- along with the union treaty and the laws passed by the Union government -- would restructure inter-republican relations. Russia was leading this process. This was part of the reconstruction of the USSR as a federation, a painful process.

The political explanation attributes a radical tinge to it by viewing it as a political instrument that aimed at transforming centre-periphery relations in the Soviet Union (Motyl, 1991; Willerton, 1990). The republics were cooperating with one another in order to augment their collective strength. Willerton believes, inter-republican cooperation originated as a form of politics in a very chaotic period of Soviet history; the republican leaders closed ranks to oppose 'national directives and preferences'. Motyl perceives the republics as forming a block, united against the Union government. It was, for him, cooperation against the central government.

The literature reviewed above captures the process of inter-republican cooperation at a very early stage of development when data were difficult to come by. It has not treated Russia's actions as a separate set of manoeuvres important in itself. But the key assumption implicit in the literature -- Russia was acting as one of the republics -- nonetheless helps structure my analysis.

The assumption that the Russian Republic was acting like another republic is intriguing. It is in line with the view of some prominent authors who noted that a large number of Russians felt their country was being governed by a spiritually alien communist leadership which was presiding over the destruction of the Russian past, intellectual heritage, and environment.[6] But Russia also formed the core of a state that governed these republics against their will. Russia and the Russians were a key component in the Soviet scheme of governance. The Communist Party of the Soviet Union (CPSU) was a Russian dominated party. Russian second secretaries watched over the non-Russian republican first secretaries (Bialer, 1986). Large numbers of Russians settled in the republics, in some cases threatening the national identities of the republics. The Soviet regime made sustained attempts to culturally Russify the non-Russian republics. As one Russian observer noted, Russia was not just another republic, Russia was the centre (Migranian, September 20, 1990, p. 3). Soviet economic and political life was dominated by the Russians (Bettelheim, 1976). Such characteristics of the Soviet state points at the need to study Russia's cooperative strategy on its own and look at it taking such features of the Soviet state into consideration.

There is another reason why a different type of study of Russian cooperation should be attempted; this also stems from the nature of the Soviet state and the transformation it was undergoing during the Gorbachev period. At the time Russia initiated its campaign for horizontal republican relations and republican sovereignty, the Soviet Union -- the centralized political behemoth, was coming apart. Many referred to this as the dissolution of an empire. Numerous scholars considered the Soviet Union to be an empire.[7] Since the emerging Russian state was entangled in this collapse of an empire, whether this process exerted any influence on the Russian governing elite should be taken into account. These two interconnected aspects of the Soviet state, Russian dominance and the imperial character, have to be present in any explanatory scheme of Russian cooperation which seemed paradoxical at the time.

The absence of any analysis of Russia's inter-republican politics prompted my research on the subject. The Russian Republic's cooperation was one of the most significant features of politics of the late Soviet period, just before the dissolution of the Soviet state. A study of this important political actor's interactions with the other republics will illuminate the formative, difficult period in the life of the newly independent countries in the process helping to explain and comprehend the sluggish development of

Introduction 7

the Commonwealth of Independent States (CIS). Such an analysis will also serve to predict the direction in which the CIS will be moving.

Notes

1. It is true Solchanyk's article deals with Russian-Ukrainian relations but he looked at them not as inter-republican cooperation, rather as a Russian attempt to redefine its ties with Ukraine and the difficulty involved in it. See Solchanyk, Roman (1992), 'Ukraine, the (former) Center, Russia, and "Russia"', *Studies in Comparative Communism*, vol. 25, no. 1, pp. 31-45.

2. For these two groups see Tolz, Vera (1990), *The USSR's Emerging Multiparty System*, Praeger, Westport; *Moscow Domestic Service* (January 20, 1991), 'Officials Cited on Baltic Russian Events'; translated in *FBIS* (January 22, 1991), pp. 104-5.

3. *Ekho Litvy* (April 17, 1990), 'Text of Baltic Economic Cooperation Agreements', pp. 1, 2; translated in *FBIS* (May 2, 1990), pp. 85-7. Also see *TASS* (May 10, 1990), 'Baltics Establish Direct Agricultural Ties'; published in *FBIS* (May 10, 1990), p. 69.

4. *Pravda* (January 16, 1991), 'Yeltsin's UN Appeal, Army Idea Criticized', p. 2; translated in *FBIS* (January 17, 1991), p. 81. The terms, treaties of inter-state relations, treaties of general cooperation, and treaties on the bases of inter-state relations are used interchangeably.

5. On non-governmental cooperation see, Kagarlitsky, Boris (1990), *Farewell Perestroika: A Soviet Chronicle*, Verso, New York; Kux, Stephen (1990), *Soviet Federalism: A Comparative Perspective*, The Institute for East-West Security Studies, New York; Otto, Robert (1990), 'Review Essay: Contemporary Russian Nationalism', *Problems of Communism*, vol. 39, no. 6, pp. 96-105; Senn, Alfred (1990), *Lithuania Awakening*, University of California Press, Berkeley; Tolz, Vera (1990), *The USSR's Emerging Multiparty System*, Praeger, Westport.

6. On this see Carrere d'Encausse, Helene (1993), *The End of the Soviet Empire: The Triumph of the Nations*, Basic Books, New York.

7. Lapidus, Gail, Zaslavsky, Victor, Goldman, Philip (1992), 'Introduction: Soviet Federalism -- Its Origins, Evolution, and Demise' in Gail Lapidus,

Victor Zaslavsky, and Philip Goldman (eds), *From Union to Commonwealth: Nationalism and Separatism in the Soviet Republics*. These three authors, while discussing emergence of Russian nationalism, refer to the withdrawal of the Russian state from the 'empire' although there were supporters of the empire inside Russia. Ronald Suny in 'State, Civil Society, and Ethnic Cultural Consolidation in the USSR -- Roots of the National Question', published in the same book contrasts 'empire' which was the Soviet Union with a multinational state in the following sentence (p. 22), 'Nations have emerged within the empire, and in that emergence the empire has begun to die. After the coup in August 1991, it appears unlikely that it will miraculously spring back to life, or in its death agony transform itself into a new democratic multinational state'. Notice Victor Zaslavsky's statement (p. 71) from his 'The Evolution of Separatism in Soviet Society under Gorbachev', also published in the same book, 'Whereas the deepening economic crisis has undermined the super power status of the Soviet Union, the nationality crisis was the main threat to the survival of the Soviet empire'. Also see Reddaway, Peter (November 7, 1991), 'The End of the Empire', *New York Review of Books*, pp. 53-9. For Reddaway, the breakup of the Soviet Union was an instance of quick dissolution of an empire. This high speed at which the empire broke up was going to be the cause of problems in the states which formerly constituted the empire. See Simes, Dimitri (1991), 'Gorbachev's Time of Troubles', *Foreign Policy*, vol. 82, pp. 97-118.

2 Theoretical Orientation and Research Design

Theoretical orientation

Cooperative processes are usually studied using theories of cooperation. This study will depart from that pattern for important reasons, some inkling of which has already been provided. Regional cooperation and coalition theories could be considered for studying the phenomenon. But regional cooperation occurs among actors who are independent states. The political actors here including Russia were not recognized states in the realm of nation states. They wanted to be independent states but had not yet become so. The degree of difference between them and independent states was too large for regional cooperation theory to be appropriate.

Similarly, the fact that they were emerging states trying to define their existence in a turbulent atmosphere rules out the use of any variation of the coalition theory. Coalition theory can analyse why coalitions are formed, how they are maintained, and how changes in power relations within a coalition take place.[1] The theory does all this when a relatively stable political environment persists. It cannot handle processes that were occurring against the background of a disintegrating state. The cooperative activities under study here were occurring in a state in which the ruling political party was thrown into disarray by the leadership's reform policy, the army was fragmenting on ethnic lines, and a rival elite was becoming ensconced in the most important republic. Moreover, this rival elite was trying to undermine the governing central authority as well. The political atmosphere prevailing in the Soviet Union renders coalition theory almost useless to study Russia's inter-republican politics. I argue that because the RSFSR's cooperation occurred in the interfacing of major political events like the disintegration of the Soviet state and fragmentation of the old Soviet elite, a combination of two theories should be used to explain this interaction process. The theories are theories of elite and empires.

Elite theory is very broad and general. It encompasses numerous variations. Those variations are used to investigate different aspects of elite behaviour. Elite recruitment studies, for instance, attempt to understand the nature of the political system and changes therein by focusing on the elite recruitment process and its change (Harasymiew, 1984; Rutland, 1991). Some have investigated patron-client relations among elites, especially their utility in providing stability in the highly uncertain world of politics (Willerton, 1992). Elite circulation or mobility across hierarchies constitutes an important element in the elite literature (Urban, 1988). The importance of the issue of redemocratization and democratic consolidation in the formerly authoritarian Asian, Latin American, and Southern European countries is making elite 'settlement' and elite 'convergence' theories popular these days (Burton, Gunther, and Higley, 1992; Gunther, 1992).

One variation of elite theory which I use here is the elite conflict theory. The literature is rich enough though not abundant. The contours of the theory are not well developed although a number of generalizations can be detected. Authors have written on the causes of elite conflict and divisions, modes and consequences of such conflicts.

The Russian governing elite emerged as a rival of the Soviet central elite. This elite had much more liberal views as regards economic and political reforms. Ready to concede that the old relations between the centre and the republics could not be preserved because of the upsurge of nationalism in the republics, it wanted to weaken the central government by offering the republics status of independent states. But at the same time, the RSFSR political elite was Russian and, consequently, it wanted to manage the breakup in a manner so the Russians would not lose too much.

The concept of 'elite conflict' has long been present in political discourse but with ill defined boundaries. It has been used to mean divisions on issues manifested in votes cast in the legislature (Smith, 1974). Lack of agreement on matters such as the status of the church in the state or how inclusive politics should be (whether the Communist Party should be allowed to function openly) as happened during the Spanish transition to democracy has been defined as elite conflict (Gunther, 1992).

But most of the time the concept of elite conflict has been used as a more potent term than just divisions on issues. Thus elite conflict has come to signify acute tension and the resultant serious rift among members of the elite. In such a conflict, rival elite groups are engaged in eliminating, seriously weakening each other, or abandoning the erstwhile allies. In Lachman's (1990; 1989) view, elite conflict is a war in which one segment of the elite tries to eliminate the other. He applied his elite conflict model to the English civil war in the seventeenth century and explained it as a conflict between the horizontal absolute monarchy and the local lords. The elite conflict which we have labelled the Cultural Revolution in China was a leftist war waged by Mao and his followers against the moderate party leaders (Liao, 1984). The effort by the reformers in the ruling Institutional Revolutionary Party (PRI) of Mexico to marginalize traditional party elites by taking state resource distribution out of their control is also a manifestation of elite conflict (Fox, 1994). It is in this more restricted sense that I use the term -- as a deep chasm leading to serious struggle to undermine or destroy the rival.

Because elite conflict is a cut-throat struggle among the governing elite, it usually occurs in times of major changes. Iranian politics was rife with elite conflict in the immediate aftermath of the revolution. The secular elements tried to sideline the clergy in the emerging political system using legal means but lost out and were themselves banished from politics (Malek, 1989). Earlier in Spain, fissures among the elite appeared after the modernization effort of Primo de Rivera resulted in major socio-economic transformations (Ben-Ami, 1990).

It is the writings on democratic transition from military authoritarian regimes that has drawn renewed attention to elite conflict and has more relevance for this study. According to one version of the argument, democratization is always preceded by cracks in the authoritarian government following which the soft-liners abandon the authoritarian scheme (O'Donnell and Schimitter, 1986). As another version puts it, the democratization process gathers force as divisions among the governing elite leads to a group from it joining groups outside the regime (Przeworski, 1988). The democratization process started by Gorbachev and the elite conflict that later surfaced and is in the centre of this study exerted reciprocal influences.

Soviet type societies tended to be prone to elite conflict. The Soviet Union itself experienced such conflicts at different levels, national, regional, and local (Clarke, 1992). The Tenth Party Congress of the CPSU tried to outlaw them. But they continued behind public view; a major one caused Khrushchev's ouster. It was not until the Gorbachev period that such struggles were to openly erupt. But the nature of these battles have changed. They used to be often violent in the period of high elite integration but became non-violent and no longer ended in the physical annihilation of the vanquished in the more recent past marked by low elite integration.[2]

As we shall see, the ouster of Boris Yeltsin from the leadership of the CPSU translated into the departure of part of the 'left' forces of *Perestroika*. The departing elite regrouped and later formed the government of Russia, becoming ensconced in the largest and most important Soviet republic from which they would deepen the conflict.

Which elite conflict?

The theme of elite division and conflict runs through numerous writings on the Gorbachev period for obvious reasons (Hill, 1991; Moltz, 1993; Roeder, 1993). It was a time characterized by fractures in different joints of the elite. I focus on a particular rupture -- the one epitomized by the Gorbachev-Yeltsin divorce. But before plunging into the subject, I will clarify how I am going to use the term 'elite' in the Soviet context.

I use this term in the sense it is usually employed in the discipline as well as Soviet studies. By elite I mean political or governing elite. Those who have more political resources at their disposal (Lane, 1988, p. 4). They are people with decision making or policy making power at different levels of a political system. In the Soviet Union, claims to elite status were grounded in officials' higher status in the party.[3] Party members holding positions in the party could be termed elites. Thus, the members of the Politburo, Central Committee (CC), republican and regional party secretaries, and officials in the Central Committee departments were elites in a narrower sense. In a broader sense, incumbents of nomenklatura positions were elites. The Soviet political elite was a melded socio-politico-economic elite because the directors of industrial plants, research institutes, or production associations tended to be party officials.[4] I consider a person to be a member of the Soviet political elite if he was a party official, a high level government official, e.g., minister, occupied a position extremely likely to be a nomenklatura position, or held a position traditionally occupied by important party members -- e.g., chairman or deputy chairman of a USSR Supreme Soviet Commission.

The Russian elite was still in the process of formation. By the term Russian elite I mean the president, members of the Russian parliament and Russian Council of Ministers, advisors to the president, and so forth.

Early writings on the Gorbachev-Yeltsin friction tended to downplay the issue seeing it as the departure of a courageous, maverick politician.[5] But Yeltsin was not a maverick fighting the system alone. He was an important member of the Soviet elite. Coming from the provincial Sverdlovsk (Yekaterinburg) he became CC Secretary for the Construction

Industry, a candidate member of the Politburo and Moscow Party First Secretary. He had developed a patronage network in Sverdlovsk where he was the Party First Secretary for a long time and picked up allies in Moscow during his tenure.[6] To give an example, Mikhail Poltoranin, editor-in-chief of *Moskovskaya Pravda*, cast his lot with Yeltsin after Yeltsin was relieved from duties by the Moscow City Party Committee; later Poltoranin became RSFSR Minister of Information and Media.

After his ouster from the Politburo and the Moscow Party Committee, Yeltsin survived more than two years in the tumultuous political environment not because caring Russian women's offer to send him home-made jams kept him going, as he would have us believe. It was partly because *Perestroika* brought about many political changes, and partly, some members of the Soviet political elite went with him and, among the rest, many sympathized with his position. Some of them undoubtedly were members of his patronage network, while the rest were not. These were the individuals who later formed the Russian government after the republican elections in Spring, 1990. Yeltsin alludes to these supporters when he writes that after his speech to the October 1987 plenum many CC members came to him and reproached him for not informing them beforehand -- they said, they could have spoken as a group (Yeltsin, 1990). During the 19th Party Conference, when Yeltsin was trying to speak and the party was manoeuvring to prevent him, many conference participants wanted Yeltsin not to leave the hall because he would not be allowed back in to speak (Yeltsin, 1990, p. 173).

The vehemence with which he was denounced at the October 1987 CC plenum after his speech is revealing. Accusations that he wanted to split the party were hurled at him. He was forced to deny he wanted to split the Central Committee (Morrison, 1991, pp. 60-73). Later research has confirmed that he seriously contemplated dividing the CPSU and forming a 'left' faction under his leadership. Indeed, Yeltsin came tantalizingly close to capturing the Russian Communist Party when his close associate and protege, Oleg Lobov, lost his bid for leadership of this party by a narrow margin (Dunlop, 1993, pp. 49-50). Yeltsin remained politically alive and an alternative elite took shape around him in Russia. The Russian government was formed with members of the Soviet elite. **Appendix A** gives background information on the members of the first Russian Council of Ministers formed after Spring, 1990 elections under Prime Minister Ivan Silaev.

Appendix A contains information on twenty eight of the thirty nine members of the Russian Council of Ministers under Silaev. Data could not be found on the past occupation of S. Ivchenko, V. Kalinin, and M. Maley. The data on G. Fil'shin, I. Gavrilov, and Yu. Solomin do not clearly indicate whether they were part of the elite. It is very likely that Fil'shin was a member of the Soviet elite because he was a departmental director in the Institute for the Economy and Industrial Organization, part of the Siberian branch of the Soviet Academy of Sciences (Chiesa and Northorp, 1993, pp. 138-9). The rest of the ministers, twenty one out of thirty nine were definitely part of the Soviet elite.

Three of them, V. Bulgak, I. Silaev, and V. Vozhakov were from the very top of the Union administrations. Silaev was a deputy chair of the USSR Council of Ministers and a member of the CC, CPSU. One of them, V. Yefimov was a RSFSR minister. Two of them were RSFSR deputy ministers. G. Kulik, the first deputy prime minister, was a veteran of the Russian agro-industrial complex as well as a member of the Central Committee of the RSFSR Communist Party. Yu. Skokov came from the military-industrial sector who was offered a position in the CC of the RSFSR Communist party at the same time he was nominated a RSFSR vice premier. The rest of the ministers were either directors of associations, chairs or deputy chairs of USSR Supreme Soviet Commissions, or CC CPSU or USSR Ministry staffers, all of them without doubt members of the Soviet elite. Other than these ministers, Yeltsin's associate and deputy in the parliament, Ruslan Khasbulatov was the leader of his university's Komsomol during his student life. After Gorbachev became CPSU leader, Khasbulatov became a member of the Scientific Council of the USSR Council of Ministers' Committee for Social Development.[7]

The overwhelmingly technical background of the RSFSR ministers indicates that the technocratic reform oriented elements of the Soviet elite were drawn to Yeltsin because he and they preferred quicker and deeper reform whereas Gorbachev wanted to proceed slowly and often seemed not progressive enough. Gorbachev's economic legislations were either not far reaching or contained conservative traps. He was painfully slow in addressing the issues of ownership and creation of a capital market (Hanson, 1992). This elite split bore resemblance to the ones postulated by theorists of democratic transitions. The elite abandoned the CPSU in reality, if not formally, in the name of democratization and economic reform. The changes in the society made it possible for them to ally with the Russian democratic forces, especially Democratic Russia. Yeltsin had cultivated relations with some leading democrats during his Congress days in 1989. The Russian government, especially Yeltsin, received support from Democratic Russia in the Russian parliament.

The rift also had the imprint of an important feature of Soviet politics; it manifested signs of patron-client politics in the Soviet Union. Many with political power now in Russia had some kind of relation with Yeltsin when he was party chief in Sverdlovsk or Moscow. As one of his aides put it, 'But to my mind, it is only natural that the formerly disgraced leader was followed by people from the Urals and Siberia' (New Times, 1991, p. 45). This group has been referred to as the Sverdlovsk mafia by some analysts (Rahr, 1992, p. 33; Sakwa, 1993, p. 51). The Sverdlovsk followers clustered around him as aides and later some of them were appointed to high posts. **Appendix B** contains a list of such officials; it is not exhaustive. Gennady Burbulis became first deputy prime minister in late 1991, before that he was the republican secretary of state. Oleg Lobov, who had worked closely with Yeltsin since the 1960s became deputy premier in July, 1991. Sergei Shakray was more an ally than a client. He was a leading member of the Russian parliament in his own right. Lev Sukhanov is one of those who preferred Yeltsin's reform policy and joined him and certainly helped Yeltsin remain afloat in the turbulent waters of Soviet politics. He has been referred to as the construction committee apparachik in a *Moscow News* article (Mikhalskaya and Orlov, July 30-August 5, 1993, p. 6).

The elite conflict which began with Yeltsin's ouster from the Moscow City Party Committee intensified with the Russian elite initiating its policy of inter-republican cooperation which aimed at supplanting the central government from centre-periphery relations and casting Russia in the role of the dominant actor on the Soviet political scene. This Russian policy was undercutting the centre's authority because it was preferable to the republics and thus much better than the central government's policy toward the republics. The Gorbachev leadership adamantly opposed republican demands for independence. True, it was giving economic autonomy to them by extending the law on the Baltic republics to the rest of the Soviet Union, but complete independence remained out of the question. The law on secession made getting out extremely difficult. The centre demonstrated its feelings on the issue by imposing an economic blockade on Lithuania after it declared independence. Gorbachev was trying to create a federation on the Western model.[8] The USSR was to have a strong centre as well as strong republics. It was not until April, 1991, and mainly because of the success of Russia's inter-republican politics that Gorbachev started to relent.

Empire in collapse

Elite conflict was part of what was happening in the Soviet Union. The Soviet state that had thus far maintained strict control over its periphery was coming unstuck as the nationalist movements in the different republics fast gained momentum. A theory of disintegration of states or break-up of empires could be combined with elite conflict theory to capture all the dimensions of the process. I have drawn upon the literature on dissolution of empires for a number of reasons.

It is true that some regarded the Soviet Union as a multinational state but more scholars thought it was an empire rather than just a multinational state. The control mechanism used to keep the periphery subdued were not different from those used in empires. The nationalist struggles in the periphery tried to free the republics from essentially imperial control in the manner that the colonies of the now defunct empires tried to free themselves. There is a practical reason as well.

It is hard to come by a concrete theory of disintegration of multinational states. Few states have broken up despite the fact that states in the international system are mostly multinational. Only four such states, other than the Soviet Union, have disintegrated: Czechoslovakia, Ethiopia, Pakistan, and Yugoslavia. Rounaq Jahan (1972) has treated Pakistan's disintegration in her book. But hers was not an attempt at theory building. Disintegration of Yugoslavia and Czechoslovakia has taken place so recently that writings on the subject have not yet caught up with events. Sri Lanka and India seem to be proceeding on the path to disintegration but have not completed the process yet.

It is not only Sovietologists who have talked about the Soviet Union as an empire but scholars who generally write on empires have done so as well. Writing in 1990 Darwin (p. 122) comments,

> The disintegration of complex imperial systems invariably defies prediction. To test the truth of this we need look no further than the events unfolding from the end of the 1980s in Eastern Europe and the Soviet Union.

Theories of empires are more theories of origin, maintenance, and logic of empires (Wolfgang, 1981). There are fewer theories on why empires declined and ended, what the ending really meant, and how the breakup process influenced the behaviour of government decision makers. It is the theories of end of empires that have the potential to be of help in explaining Russia's cooperation, an important pattern of elite behaviour occurring at the time.

Marxist, non-Marxist, and non-Marxist dialectical works have been done on the end of imperialism. Both traditional Marxist and neo-Marxist dependency scholars have written on the demise of the imperialist states. Of the more traditional Marxist theorists, Lenin has explained the end of empires as the result of the struggle of the masses of the colonies. The revolution to overthrow capitalism begin in the weaker links of capitalism (Lenin, 1926).

The neo-Marxists have given what is known as the peripheral theory of the dissolution of empires. They think imperialism has not ended, only a shift has occurred. The internationalization of capital in the form of multinational corporations did not require direct control of the peripheral countries. And there was the need to give independence to the more moderate nationalist leaders in order to forestall takeovers by radical nationalists and real change in the periphery. What is flaunted as the end of empires is nothing but a mere change of form, not content (Baran, 1957; Wallerstein, 1979).

The non-Marxist dialectical analysis is similar to the Marxist approach. It stresses the fact that it is not only capitalism or capitalist states which have been imperialist.[9] This approach resembles the neo-Marxist interpretation in its postulate that imperialism does not end but continues. It differs from the neo-Marxist perspective in the form of analysis, viewing as it does the continuity as a synthesis of the dialectics of emancipation struggles of the peripheries and attempts at further penetration by the empire. The empire needs to penetrate in order for it to maintain control and deepen exploitation. Accordingly, selective modernization becomes unavoidable. The native intelligentsia develops and frames the demand for emancipation in terms of the ideas held sacred by the imperial rulers, for instance liberty, equality.[10] But the empire changes, its form of domination changes. The struggle for independence does not completely free the nation.

Of the non-Marxist theories, John Darwin's (1991) theoretical synthesis on the breakup of the British empire is of particular interest. His work is especially relevant in the Soviet case because like the Soviet Union, the British empire collapsed rapidly. The British empire also gave birth to a Commonwealth. Its breakup has been almost non-violent like that of the USSR.

Darwin believes, the Socio-politico-economic theory, economic theory, international political theory, and nationalist struggle theory of breakdown of the British empire have to be interwoven. He proposes a synthetic interpretation. According to him, the British empire broke up because the economic decline ensuing from the second World War made it impossible to maintain high defence expenditures. In addition, the rise of the two super powers overshadowing Britain as a world power combined with the unexpectedly creative and intense nationalist struggle in the colonies to bring down the empire.

More important than this interpretation of the breakdown provided by Darwin is his conceptualization of the way it broke up or an aspect of that. Darwin argues that the British did not want to completely dismantle the empire. They wanted to create a British centred world of independent states in which British economic interests would be safeguarded and promoted, its political and cultural influence remaining intact. The result was the British Commonwealth (Darwin, 1991, p. 114).

It was the dynamics of international politics, the desire of the newly independent states to gain and maintain genuine independence, and the new direction that European politics was moving in that rendered the British Commonwealth meaningless a decade or so later as a structure of dominance. Darwin's theoretical formulations are relevant to this study as other theories of collapse of empires are to put the period and the events characteristic of the breakup of the Soviet Union into perspective.

There are other theories of collapse of empires which to some extent are incorporated in the approaches reviewed above.[11] For the purpose of this study, these three approaches and the ideas gleaned from them are sufficient.

The theories of the breakup of empires help to understand and conceptualize the way this tumultuous period in Soviet history was influencing the process of cooperation. There has been cooperation among ethnic groups against the ethnic enemy before.[12] But the dynamics of those processes were different because the nature of the states was different from that of the Soviet state.

The view that the Russians who ruled the USSR would try to retain their imperial advantages seems attractive because of its appeal to common sense and our collective experience as the people of this century which has witnessed the apparent dismantling of the last empires. But there are precedents that divisions among imperial elites led to the relinquishment of imperial ambitions by elements of the imperial elites and their joining the anti-imperial movements (Galtung, Heiestad, and Ruge, 1979).

The use of theory of empires allows me to ask the second question posed at the very beginning. Not only that, some new findings may come out of the study which will answer the following questions: did the elite conflict simmering in the system force the Russians to take a much softer approach so that in the Soviet case the victory of the nationalists is more substantial? In other words, were the nationalist movements able to exploit the elite conflict to their advantage? A modification of the theory of breakup of empires might be necessary.

Primary research questions

This analysis centres around the following questions:

1. Why did the RSFSR engage in cooperation with other republics?

Theoretical orientation 19

2. What were the different forms of cooperation that it engaged in?
3. How did the process of disintegration of the Soviet Union affect the Russian Republic's cooperation?

The first question attempts to uncover causal links among the forms of cooperative actions and elite motivation. The second question is more descriptive in nature because it is about the kind of activities involved. Cooperation is a general, abstract term, its components are specific activities. a study of all kinds of actions which constituted this process we prefer to call cooperation has not been done yet. The aim of the second question is to generate such a study as part of the book.

Theories of breakdowns of empires inform the third question. The Russian government was the government of the dominant ethnic group which was practically becoming the legitimate government of Russia. Its interactions with the governments of the imperial state's rebellious periphery must be related with the tectonic shifts occurring in the empire. This question tries to reflect that aspect of the events.

The theses

My theses are grounded in elite and empire theories and they take into consideration developments occurring in the Soviet Union at the time. I have identified that time frame as June 1990-August 1991.

> Thesis 1. Through its policy of cooperation, Russia attempted to render the central government irrelevant in centre-periphery relations.

The first thesis is the central assumption. I take the position in this study that an alliance of market oriented, democratic, anti-Gorbachev, forces came together around Boris Yeltsin in 1989-90. By early 1990, this alliance inside the Russian Republic started using some strategies against the Gorbachev government. One of the strategies was propaganda to the effect that the Gorbachev leadership did not have any control over the situation in the country, was very unpopular with the people, and was turning away from reform (Hough, 1990). Yet another strategy was to initiate a policy of creating and implementing a more liberal structure of relations among the republics of the Soviet Union. The result of this policy was Russia's cooperative interactions. Later, the democratic alliance adopted other strategies as well, for example, the creation of the Russian presidency, and getting Yeltsin elected to it.[13]

Some examples of actions performed by Russia can further illustrate the basis of the first thesis in what was happening at the time. The RSFSR was being supportive of Latvia at a time when Latvia was declaring that it would not uphold union programmes at the cost of 350 million rubles.[14] The Russian leaders were declaring their support for the republics' aspirations for independence at a time when Lithuania was being pressured by the USSR about sending its young to the Soviet army and refusing to comply.[15] Also, Estonia was agreeing to pay only 160 million rubles whereas the USSR wanted 732 million. The Estonian government was saying it would not give a kopek into the fund for stabilization, and the fund for compensation.

The Russian governmental elites emerged in 1990 as an alternative elite and, in its effort to gain power, it was exposing the central government as impotent, unimaginative, and without any influence with the republics. This thesis not only reflects the 'cunning' aspect of the situation, it also brings out the precarious nature of events going on. The Russian elites were conceding that the demands for independence by the republics and the economic decline of the Soviet Union would not allow holding the union together in the old form. They felt the Gorbachev government was not sensitive to this. Another way of looking at the thesis is: the Gorbachev leadership which was still associated with the older governing party and ideology, however modified, was not able to cross the crucial threshold.[16] This the Russian Republic was willing to do.[17]

> Thesis 2. Russia was cooperating with the other republics to salvage, as much as possible, the older relations with the republics which existed before the turmoil started.

The second thesis is derived from the theories of dissolution of empires. The Russian Republic did not join the block of rebellious republics to maintain the existing economic relations and to increase its autonomy just like another republic. It was not, as I already pointed out, just another republic. It was not helping the other republics out of pure idealist conception of nations' right to independence and self-determination.

The theories of empires suggest that empires, at the stage of collapse, usually try to salvage as much as possible from the wreckage. Was the Russian government trying to do the same? Its policy might have been: we (the Russian Republic leaders) will support their (the republics') demand for independence, but retain them in a Russia centred world like the British Commonwealth which was intended to be a British dominated, British centred political, economic, cultural world of influence for Britain.

Thesis 3. The cooperation process engaged in by Russia was a package of political, economic, socio-cultural, and security related interactions.

I infer the cooperation process formed a whole. It was not sometimes political and sometimes economic. In other words, 1990 was not the year of economic activities and 1991 that of political because the situation deteriorated further. From the beginning, it was a political process in essence -- a set of different kinds of interactions performed to achieve political ends, not a purely economic goal or a technical one.[18] The third thesis tries to represent this idea.

The Russian government took it on itself to peacefully reconstruct a structure of more liberal relations. In a state boiling over with tension, the Russian elites' decision was, through policy offers and legal means, to out manoeuvre the central government.

Research approach, method, and organization

The book will entail both quantitative and qualitative research. Along with the definition of the term, cooperation, this section presents a brief discussion of the research approach and method. I also lay out the chapter organization of the book.

For the purpose of collecting data, the term 'cooperation' has been defined more clearly. It means interactions between the Russian government and the governments of other republics to establish or expand political, economic, military, or cultural ties. The term also incorporates Russia's actions to support the goals of its partner (in this case another republic). The action must be spontaneously performed by the Russian government and not under duress exerted by the central government or at the request of the central government. The action must be performed by the Russian government or a representative thereof. Such an expansive definition of cooperation is needed in view of the time at which it took place. The circumstances were such that any non-hostile interactions were going to contribute towards the restructuring of centre-periphery relations. Given below are some examples of actions which have been counted as cooperative actions.

1. Any treaty or agreement signed by the Russian government with another republic.
2. Making a statement promoting the republics' demands for independence.

Announcing support for a particular republic, when it was opposing the centre's policies. Making declarations that Russia supported the leadership of a republic in its demand for independence.
3. Writing letters to the leaders of republics. Receiving letters from them.
4. Telephone conversation with republican leaders.

I study the Russian Republic's cooperative actions taking place during the period from June, 1990 to August, 1991. There are a number of reasons for selecting this time. The Russian government began working in June, 1990. It is this government which was formed by the alternative elite. After the coup took place in August, 1991, the dynamics of Soviet politics changed. The central government of the Communist Party became irrelevant, and for all practical purposes, the USSR had disintegrated.

Content analysis

I conducted a content analysis to see if the first thesis is supported. This thesis postulates that Russia used cooperation to render the union government meaningless by offering and practicing more liberal centre-periphery relations. This thesis should find support if it can be shown that the Russian elites themselves thought their cooperation aimed at this goal. For the first thesis I undertook a content analysis of public pronouncements of elites.

Legal analysis

To see if Russia was trying to retain as much influence as possible (the second thesis), I did a treaty analysis. I collected and analysed the most important treaties, the ones on the bases of inter-state relations Russia signed with the other republics. I desired to learn whether they contain restrictive articles or clauses that are more beneficial to Russia than the republics, or that would limit the independence of a nation state. Treaties are international legal materials which have to be analysed following particular methods. Using those methods I analysed these core treaties.

Events data analysis

To see if the third thesis which stipulates that the process of cooperation was a total package of different genres of actions held up, I collected events data or cooperative action data. A number of primary sources such as Russian and republican newspapers and the proceedings of the Russian parliament were used to gather the transaction data. The interaction data (agreements, letters etc.) will show whether only economic interactions took place or there were other kinds of cooperation and how they related to one another. I also used these data to see if they support the first and second theses. The events data can demonstrate whether the way Russia was trying to support the republics' independent actions was buying it more and more leverage in the political struggle going on in the USSR. Not only that, they will help to show if it was trying to protect imperial interests in a more lenient manner.

Case study

I also did a case study of Russia's cooperation with Lithuania during the same period. The case study has been done to get a clearer picture of the larger context -- to see whether the miniature gives the same understanding of the broader phenomenon. This is a two part case study. The first part focuses on the interactions and their peculiar features, if any. The second one studies how Lithuania was helped by Russia's actions in asserting its position against the centre.

Organization

In the third chapter I present the interaction data with an analysis thereof. I also try to find out in this chapter whether the events data support the arguments contained in both theses one and two. Chapters four and five contain the case study. The content analysis is presented in chapter six. The treaties are analysed in the seventh chapter. The style of presentation follows the manner in which cooperation processes unfold. In such processes visits, meetings, negotiations, and statements climax in the signing of treaties or agreements. In the concluding chapter, I discuss what conclusions can be drawn from the data, how that affect the theses, what the theoretical and practical implications of this research are.

Notes

1. For writings on coalition behaviour see, Laver, Michael., and Higgins, Michael (1986), 'Coalition or Fianna Fail? The Politics of Inter-Party Government in Ireland' in Pridham, Geoffrey (ed.), *Coalition Behaviour in Theory and Practice*, Cambridge University Press, London, pp. 171-97; also in the same book, Gleiber, Dennis. 'Cabinet Stability in the French Fourth Republic: The Ramadier Coalition Government of 1947' pp. 93-116; Broadbent, Jeffrey (1989), 'Strategies and Structural Contradictions: Growth Coalition Politics in Japan', *American Sociological Review*, vol. 54, no. 5, pp. 707-21.

2. For the terms 'high integration' and 'low integration' see Lane, David (1988), 'Elites and Political Power in the USSR' in Lane, David (ed.), *Elites and Political Power in the USSR*, Edward Elgar Publishing Ltd., Aldershot, p. 14; For the change in the nature of conflict see, Welsh, William (1979), *Leaders and Elites*, Rinehart and Winston, New York.

3. For a discussion of the subject see, Rigby, T.H. (1990), *Political Elites in the USSR: Central Leaders and Local Cadres from Lenin to Gorbachev*, Edward Elgar Publishing Ltd., Aldershot, pp. 12-42. He believes all party members can be considered elites in the broadest sense of the term. I use the term in a narrower sense.

4. See Harasymiew (1984), op. cit., ch. 7. On directors of educational, research institutes being scholar-administrator party officials see Malcolm, Neil (1988), 'Foreign Affairs Specialists and Decision Makers' in Lane, David (ed.), op. cit.

5. Bialer thought it was the departure of a colourful politician from Gorbachev's team which would not seriously affect the reform project. See Bialer, Seweryn (1989), 'The Yeltsin Affair: the Dilemma of the Soviet Left in Gorbachev's Revolution' in Bialer, Seweryn (ed.), *Politics, Society, and Nationality Inside Gorbachev's Russia*, Westview Press, Boulder, pp. 91-120. It should, however, be mentioned that Tismaneanu attributed more importance to it by viewing it as very much a part of the left-right conflict in the party leadership. See Tismaneanu, Vladimir (1988), 'The Yeltsin Affair', *Orbis*, vol. 32, p. 277.

6. When he was Moscow party first secretary 60% of the district party first secretaries in Moscow were ousted. See Yeltsin, Boris (1990), *Against the Grain: An Autobiography*, Jonathan Cape Ltd., London. There were

accusations that Yeltsin was placing his own people in the positions vacated, see Bialer (1989), op. cit.

7. For biographical information showing incumbents of such positions as previously held by RSFSR ministers as being party elites see biographical information of Soviet elites in Rahr, Alexander (1990), *A Biographical Directory of 100 Leading Soviet Officials*, Westview Press, Boulder. Also see Levytsky, Boris (1969), *The Soviet Political Elite*, Hoover Institution Press, Stanford.

8. On the subject of Gorbachev's policy on centre-periphery relations see, Hazard, John (1992), 'State, Law and the National Question in the USSR' in Motyl, Alexander (ed.), *The Post-Soviet Nations: Perspectives on the Demise of the USSR*, Columbia University Press, New York.

9. For this kind of analysis see Nederveen Pieterse, Jan (1990), *Empire and Emancipation: Power and Liberation on a World Scale*, Pluto Press, London.

10. The similarity has to be noticed. At the beginning of the nationalist struggle in the republics, their basis in the concept and program of *Perestroika* was emphasized by the republican leaders. See Lapidus (1992), op. cit.

11. There exist some interesting and insightful works on breakup of empires. See Smith, Tony (1981), *The Pattern of Imperialism: The United States, Great Britain, and the Late-Industrializing World since 1815*, Cambridge University Press, Cambridge. Galtung, Johan, Heiestad, Tore, and Ruge, Eric (1979), *On the Decline and Fall of Empires: The Roman Empire and Western Imperialism Compared*, The United Nations University, Japan. Especially thought-provoking is these three writers' discussion of the death of the ideology used by an empire and also their comparison of Western imperialism with non-Western imperialism.

12. There was cooperation among different ethnic groups in Burma against the dominant ethnic group; see Premdas, Ralph (ed.), (1990), *Secessionist Movements in Comparative Perspective*, St. Martin's Press, New York.

13. Urban, Michael (1992), 'Boris Yeltsin, Democratic Russia, and the Campaign for the Russian Presidency', *Soviet Studies*, vol. 44, no. 2, pp. 187-207. Urban thinks it was to Yeltsin's credit that he was able to create the Russian presidency. Of course, Yeltsin, at that time, was by no means acting alone.

14. *Ekho Litvy* (May 30, 1991), 'Riga', under 'Puls Planety', p. 1.

15. *Ekho Litvy* (May 31, 1991), 'Vnov o sluzhbe v armii', p. 1.

16. For Gorbachev's Association with the party and his view of the party's position in the political system see, Robinson, Neil (1992), 'Gorbachev and the Place of the Party in the Soviet Reform, 1985-91', *Soviet Studies*, vol. 44, no. 3, pp. 423-44.

17. Here a news item on Yeltsin campaign for the Russian presidency is relevant. Ekho Litvy reports that Yeltsin was being supported by parties and movements as a candidate for the Russian presidency who would bring about the peaceful rebirth of Russia and the Union of the sovereign republics. See *Ekho Litvy* (May 30, 1991), 'Vo Vladivostoke sozdan kraevoi kommitet v podderzhku Yeltsina', p. 4.

18. Even the purely economic actions of the Russian government were perceived by some to be essentially political. A journalist while interviewing Prunskiene, the Lithuanian Prime Minister at the time, comments that Russia's agreement with Lithuania was really helping it to hold on to its position vis a vis the central government. See *Izvestia* (August 20, 1990), 'Ot Chevo Ukhodit i Kuda Idet Litva: Beseda Nashikh Korrespondentov s Primer Ministrom Respubliki Kazimeroi Prunskiene', p.3.

3 The Flow of Interactions: The Nature of Transactions between Russia and its Partners

Introduction

Russia's cooperative interactions with the other republics began as a deliberate process of broad, general cooperation. It manifested every sign of being well thought out and all encompassing. It was not, even at the point of initiation, a narrow, single goal oriented process of cooperation. The Russian leaders were not somewhat haphazardly trying to cope with unfolding events by taking care of the most important aspect of inter-republican interactions -- inter-republican trade. Nor were they participating, as equal partners, with the other republics in a joint struggle to augment republican autonomy. The whole process, if we look at the actual interactions, looks more like an effort to mould Russia's ties with the republics into a different kind of relationship.

The Russian government elites' efforts to cooperate with the other republics of the Soviet Union also began as a broad-based government policy to reorient Russia's relations with the republics. It was the Russian parliament which instructed the newly formed Russian government to develop mutually beneficial relations with the republics right after the parliament began to function. This suggests that the policy was not the whim of some radical politicians in the government. The Russian parliament did contain some radical democrats but the majority of the members did not fall into that category.

In this chapter, I discuss the types of cooperative interactions that took place between Russia and the republics in 1990-1991. I also analyse the

28 Inter-republican cooperation

overall thrusts of Russia's policy of inter-republican cooperation arguing that the data imply that the Russian Republic had major goals which it wanted to attain through this web of cooperative relations. The events data are used to that end.

The interactions

I have collected data on the cooperative actions and interactions of the Russian Republic with the other republics. I have also collected statements made by Russian leaders supporting positions taken by other republics. The evidence has been collected from the following sources: *Ekho Litvy, Izvestia, Pravda Ukrainy, Rossiiskaya gazeta*.

Izvestia was a central (Soviet) newspaper and by 1990 had acquired a liberal outlook and was trying to give a balanced coverage of both the government and opposition actions. It published a large number of reports on inter-republican cooperation. *Rossiiskaya gazeta* was of course the official newspaper of the Russian Supreme Soviet and thus reported on Russian government actions. In addition to *Izvestia* and *Rossiiskaya gazeta*, I used the *Foreign Broadcast Information Service (FBIS)*. The *FBIS* translated a wide variety of Soviet media materials, both central and regional, and captured many republican cooperative actions. These three sources were used to obtain data on most cooperative actions of the RSFSR.

To further minimize any bias in the data, two republican newspapers were used; they were *Ekho Litvy* and *Pravda Ukrainy*, the chief newspapers from Lithuania and Ukraine.

Ekho Litvy, FBIS, Izvestia, and Pravda Ukrainy were systematically searched for information on Russia's cooperative actions for the whole period from June, 1990-August 19, 1991. *Rossiiskaya gazeta* started publishing in November, 1990; so it was searched systematically from the day it started publishing till the end of my research period. Thus *Rossiiskaya gazeta* does not cover the period from June, 1990-October, 1990. To compensate for that, I have used *Bakinskii rabochii*, the Azerbaijani newspaper for the period from June, 1990-December, 1990. Its use no way parallels the use of *Rossiiskaya gazeta* but reduces the bias somewhat. Some interactions were picked up from *Kazakhstanskaya pravda* but this newspaper was not systematically perused to gather cooperation data. I have used multiple sources to counter editorial biases. The use of a number of sources also makes the data more complete. However, it must be stressed that although an attempt was made to gather all the cooperative actions, the data do not constitute the universe of cooperative actions by Russia. The under-represented category are the meetings because some negotiation sessions must have been missed but that would not bias the data one way or the other.

The statements were made by Russian government officials, e.g. the chair of the parliament, the prime minister, on different occasions. I counted one statement per occasion although more than one was made. A representative statement was selected. In most cases, only one statement was made. The actions were grouped into different categories. **Appendix C** contains explanations of different categories.

Table 3.1
Russia's cooperation with other republics, 1990-91

Forms of Actions	Number of Actions	% of Total
Agreements	40	19
Appeals	6	3
Communications	21	10
Communiques	20	10
Declarations	7	3
Meetings	43	21
Statements	28	14
Represent Interests	2	1
Speech	2	1
Visits	23	11
Other	14	7
Total	206	100

Table 3.1 presents interactions that took place between Russia and the rest of the republics. The table shows that during the period of my research Russia engaged in two hundred and six actions in this fourteen and a half month period -- about fourteen actions per month. These were not simply signing treaties on economic relations. As a matter of fact, formal treaties constitute only 19% of the interactions. The economic treaties were a part of that 19% of written agreements.

Important treaties dealing primarily with the basis of inter-state relations including recognition of the treaty signing parties as sovereign states

30 *Inter-republican cooperation*

were signed. There were head of the state level visits, statements made in support of the republics' struggle to gain independence, declarations made condemning use of force against the republics, and appeals. Meetings to discuss new market oriented economic relations, rather than simply preserve old economic linkages were held. Visits by high level Russian government officials most of which were symbolic of Russia's willingness to recognize the republics as independent states were 11% of the total. These visits reinforced the initiation of state level relations with the republics, and served to highlight Russia's effort to make a different kind of relation work between itself and the republics, a kind the republics preferred. Russia used a good mix of activities to support the republics against the centre as well as establish close ties with them.

Table 3.2
Cooperation in 1990 and 1991

Actions	1990	1991
Agreements	18	22
Appeals	2	4
Communications	8	13
Communiques	8	12
Declarations	4	3
Meetings	18	25
Represent Interests	0	2
Speeches	2	0
Statements	13	15
Visits	10	13
Other	4	10
Total	87	119

Table 3.2 shows the pattern of activities in 1990 and 1991. The data in this table are especially significant because the distribution over time demonstrates that there was much planning and thinking that went into this policy. A little less than half the interactions took place in 1990. These

include the two major treaties on inter-state relations between Russia and Kazakhstan, and Russia and Ukraine. Almost the same numbers of agreements were signed in 1990 and 1991. Both the speeches of Yeltsin were delivered in 1990. The number of visits that took place are almost equal, ten in 1990 and thirteen in 1991. There was a perceptible increase in the number of appeals and statements and items in the 'Other' category. But the overall direction represents more a secular shift rather than a sudden and radical change. This of course is supportive of the thrust of my argument -- Russia initiated this policy of inter-republican cooperation with particular objectives in mind and did it as a well articulated policy. The Russian government began its efforts to create 'inter-state' relations immediately after coming to power, not in 1991 when it was becoming clear to many outsiders that the USSR would fall apart.

Russia interacted more with the Baltic republics and Ukraine. But it had interactions with almost all the republics in an effort to strengthen horizontal ties with all of them. Tajikistan was the only republic with which no Russian interaction was recorded either in a bilateral or multilateral setting. But it is very likely that some meetings took place.

Below I study the individual interactions grouping them into clusters on the basis of the goals they served in the overall policy.

Laying the groundwork

The government level cooperation of the Russian Republic was initiated by the Russian parliament right after the formation of the Russian government. As already noted, after being elected, the parliament instructed the Russian government to develop mutually beneficial relations with the republics. The Russian government then went ahead using the means of communications and two important visits to Latvia to signal its willingness to develop a new kind of relationship with the republics.

Yeltsin, the chair of the parliament, and the Russian premier Silaev invited the Lithuanian government to sign a treaty through a letter. They expressed their desire to widen relations with Lithuania. This was not an invitation to sign a treaty on economic relations or any particular aspect of Lithuanian-Russian relations. The proposed treaty was going to encompass all spheres of cooperation of mutual benefit in 1991 and for the future. They informed the Lithuanian government that the Russian Council of Ministers was willing to organize the work on this treaty. Yeltsin and Silaev sent out a similar invitation to the Latvian government inviting it to a dialogue. Both of these letters were written in the same month, July, 1990, less than a month after the formation of the Russian government. In another letter to Levon Ter-Petrosyan, chair of the Armenian parliament, Yeltsin emphasized the necessity to develop horizontal relations among the republics.[1]

The Azerbaijani government leaders, while negotiating a treaty with Russia, mentioned that Russian leaders Yeltsin and Silaev proposed the treaty to them.[2] Russian government officials themselves talked about Russian efforts to build relations on a new basis with the Republics.

Two major initiation steps were the two visits, one by a parliamentary delegation to Lithuania and the other by Yeltsin himself to Latvia. Both of these visits were early in terms of the time the Russian government started working. The visit by the parliamentary delegation took place in early July and the visit by Yeltsin in late July, 1990. The parliamentary delegation went to the Lithuanian parliament when it was celebrating the 70th anniversary of the treaty between Lithuania and Russia in which Russia recognized Lithuania as an independent state. The Russian delegation contained members like the chair of the Soviet of Nationalities, Ramazan Abdullatipov, and a member of the Presidium of the Russian Supreme Soviet, Nikolai Travkin. The delegation expressed the view that the Russian and Lithuanian people would preserve good neighbourly relations. This visit was to attend the celebration of Lithuania's sovereignty and implied Russian willingness to accept Lithuania as a separate state and to enter into good neighbourly relations with it.

Yeltsin's visit to Latvia, although described as a vacation at the time, was in fact an initiation effort. During this visit Russia signed a communique with the Baltic republics. In this communique all the Baltic republics agreed to sign treaties with Russia without delay. The initial agreements were to be political and legal. Yeltsin must have further clarified Russia's position on inter-republican relations during the visit and was able to get the Baltic republics to agree to sign the kind of agreements that Russia had invited the republics to sign in its letters discussed above.[3] During this visit Yeltsin also delivered a speech to the Latvian parliament. He mentioned in this speech that the treaty with Latvia would be in two parts, the first part would be political and legal, with the treaty being a general cooperation treaty (Litvinova, August 2, 1990, p. 2).

These letters and the visits were a cluster of activities which constituted the effort to initiate Russia's inter-republican politics. They took place around the same time and were signalling attempts by the Russian government. They served to communicate Russia's policy to the republics. In addition to communicating that Russia would accept the republics as independent states, Russia informed the republics that it was more interested in the construction of the political basis of the new relationship.

Recognition, close ties, and control

The legal reconstruction of Russia's relations with the fourteen other republics took mainly two forms, recognition of the republics as sovereign states and establishing very close ties with them. Russia did this by signing Treaties on the Bases of Inter-state Relations, the treaties which constituted the core of the agreements it signed with the other republics. These are the kind of political treaties that Russia wanted to sign in the first place when it invited some republics to begin dialogues.

These treaties touched upon almost all aspects of inter-state relations, e.g., political, economic, security, cultural, and minorities. Such treaties were signed with Belarus, Estonia, Kazakhstan, Kyrgyzstan, Latvia, Lithuania, Moldova, and Ukraine. It was agreed that a similar treaty would be signed between Russia and Turkmenistan. A treaty of such nature was indeed drafted with Armenia just before the coup of August 1991. Russia did invite Azerbaijan to sign such a treaty. These treaties will be analysed in greater detail in a subsequent chapter. A few words on their content and the pattern of negotiations will show that they served as formal reconfiguration of close relations with Russia.

The subjects the treaties dealt with ranged from recognition of the parties as sovereign states to recognition of the necessity to establish a collective security system.[4] They put emphasis on the minority issue; it was one of the most important topics in the treaties because a large number of Russians were living in other republics. The Kazakh-RSFSR treaty, the RSFSR-Ukraine treaty both provide for cooperation in foreign policy, in development of a common European market as well as a Eurasian market, and in creating an all-encompassing international system of ecological security. In addition to all this, the treaty signing parties would also cooperate in migration policy and fight against organized and international crime. The treaty with Moldova provided for extensive information exchange and cooperation on the issue of subversive organizations on each other's territories. These treaties tended to contain restrictive terms on the minority issues.

These broad cooperation treaties took much longer to negotiate whereas the much narrower economic agreements were hastily negotiated and signed. This indicates republican resistance. The negotiations with Lithuania began in summer, 1990, and the treaty was signed at the end of July, 1991. The same is true about Estonia and Latvia and the other republics. The process was conflict ridden too. Lithuania and Russia had a serious disagreement over the issue of citizenship of the Russian minority in Lithuania. During negotiations, Latvia withdrew at one point.[5]

34 Inter-republican cooperation

The Treaties on the Bases of Inter-State Relations were not the only agreements signed among the parties. There were economic agreements through which the RSFSR agreed to maintain the previous level of economic relations with the republics. This agreement to maintain previous economic ties reveals an interesting relation with establishment of close relations. The republican governments needed to maintain previous level of economic relations, as numerous press reports suggest about Lithuania. They needed it more than the Russian republic. It was so because the much larger size of the Russian economy made it viable.[6] *Izvestia* referred to the Lithuanian-Russian economic agreement as Russia helping Lithuania in its firm stance against the centre.[7]

Russia wanted to sign treaties defining political relations first. But it did sign a number of economic treaties with some republics so the previous level of trade could be maintained. These treaties almost always preceded the broad treaties on inter-state relations. They were quickly negotiated and signed. They contained provisions for signing treaties of much wider range, or treaties on other aspects of inter-state relations or there were communiques on the agreement to sign treaties on other subjects. The economic treaty between Lithuania and Russia was signed in the second half of August, 1990, and the two parties decided that they would sign a treaty of much broader scope.[8] The same is true in the case of Kyrgyzstan, Turkmenistan, and probably Kazakhstan. Russia signed two bilateral agreements with Turkmenistan and Kyrgyzstan on maintaining supplies at 1990 level, but at the same time they agreed to sign agreements on a whole host of issues by November the first, 1990. Fragmentary evidence suggests that Kazakhstan and the RSFSR signed a less important treaty before signing the inter-state relations treaty. This pattern of signing the narrow economic treaty first and then the inter-state relations treaty was broken with Georgia and Moldova to sign the broader treaties first.

Because of the much larger size of the Russian economy this pattern of signing the economic treaties and then the inter-state relations treaties is important. Russia clearly wanted the more general treaties signed first and it did sign them with the republics which would sign them first. But when republics resisted or who seemed likely to resist, Russia signed economic treaties first which boosted the republics' position against the centre and also extracted the promise to sign treaties of more extensive nature. One gets the impression that Russia was signing the economic treaties so that the republics would sign inter-state relations treaties later.

Tying through treaties was part of it, although an extremely important part. The transaction data also capture actions performed by Russia which had the potential to limit republican sovereignty. Russia signed a protocol with Estonia and Latvia in early 1991 providing for a special programme for the Russian speaking population in those republics. This protocol was going to be applied to Lithuania soon. This was not the only instance of an effort to establish control over republican minority policy. A delegation from the Russian Ministry of Education visited Lithuania in early May, 1991. It went there to devise a programme of literature for the Russian school children. In effect, Lithuania had ceded control over its minority education policy.

Some of the restrictive provisions of the bilateral treaties were already at work. According to the provisions of the bilateral treaties, two foreign minister level meetings were held in Riga, Latvia, in February and March of 1991, to coordinate foreign policies including relations with the USSR foreign ministry. It should be underlined that cooperation in foreign policy was important to Russia. In a meeting of the Russian and Ukrainian foreign ministers the two sides agreed to sign a protocol on their ministries' cooperation and to hold periodic meetings to coordinate foreign policy actions. Also an agreement between Belarus and Russia signed in April, 1991, stipulated that the two parties would coordinate their foreign economic activities such as joining the IMF or GATT.

After the disintegration of the Soviet Union, most republics dissociated themselves from Russia as quickly as possible (Ganyushkin, September, 1993, p. 3). In view of that fact, one can conclude that the republican leadership must have considered their having to sign treaties providing for very close relations with Russia an act that had to be performed. Russia was being forthcoming by recognizing the republics as independent countries which the centre was not willing to do. But Russia was also attaching the republics to itself with intimate ties. A Russian minister once remarked that Russia was establishing ever deeper contacts with the republics without the interference of the central government. So when the USSR collapsed the Soviet Union would be just like the British Commonwealth. [9]

Curtailing the centre's authority

It is one of the main arguments of the study that the Russian Republic's inter-republican politics aimed mainly at weakening the central government. The agreements Russia signed with the republics clearly demonstrate that inter-republican economic and other relations were taken out from the centre's jurisdiction. But aside from those broad thrusts, Russian leaders performed some actions which piecemeal took areas out of the centre's jurisdiction. In some cases it was done deliberately, in others, the central government's failure to establish control presented opportunities which were simply availed of to stabilize conflict ridden areas (e.g. Georgia).

The Russian parliament purposely tried to take away the central government's authority when it passed a resolution making it impermissible to use Russian soldiers in solving nationality problems beyond Russia's borders. One of the pretexts under which Soviet soldiers (Russian) could be used in other republics was to safeguard the rights of the Russian minority living in those republics. It was a two pronged attack on the centre's authority, first, it asserted Russian control over the military; second, it declared Russia's position on use of force in the republics.[10] The Russian leaders did mention later, after the Lithuanian incident in January, 1993, that it was against Russian law to use Russian soldiers beyond Russia's borders against republics. They interpreted the resolution which prohibited use of Russian soldiers in ethnic problems beyond Russia's borders as forbidding their use against any republican government.[11] Another deliberate attempt to cut back on the union government's authority was establishing republican control over the environment. The Russian and Ukrainian parliaments signed an agreement in November, 1990, to work together to save the environment of the Azov sea.

The complexity of the ethnic problems and the centre's inability to solve them gave Russia the opportunity to establish republican authority over such policy areas. The ethnic problems also created refugees who came to Russia and Russian leaders felt forced to act. Refugees came from South Ossetia into Russia and the Russian government felt obliged to talk to Georgia about the problem so that the problem could be solved. The result was the protocol signed between Georgia and Russia on South Ossetia. The Georgians were happy about the agreement because they found Russia lenient on the issue of the status of South Ossetia because the agreement referred to it as the former autonomous region. They agreed to ask the central government to withdraw its forces from South Ossetia because they were supplying weapons to some elements there which fuelled the conflict. This agreement provided for a joint Georgian-RSFSR force to disarm armed groups and keep order in South Ossetia. In addition, Georgia and Russia would cooperate in returning the refugees.[12]

The visit of the Russian parliamentary delegation to Azerbaijan and Moldova were also made to manage ethnic conflicts. During the visit to Moldova, the Russian government clearly said that it had to act because the central government was not doing anything appropriate about ethnic conflicts.[13]

Building, strengthening solidarity with the republics

Russia built, expressed, and strengthened solidarity with the other republics. It built solidarity by verbally supporting the republics' longing for independence and by representing the Russian Republic as one of the republics fighting on the same side.

The Russian leaders supported the desire of the republics for independence through many statements. Khasbulatov, deputy chair of the Russian parliament, said in an interview that Armenia was making excellent progress toward independence. Silaev supported the position of the republics. The cooperative posture of the Russian republic incorporated solidarity with the other republics as one of the republics. This was an attempt to portray Russia as engaged in a struggle along with the republics against the threat that the centre posed. Using various means, such as resolutions, appeals, statements, Russia showed that it identified with the republics just as another republic under the repressive rule of the centre.

This was an attempt to picture Russia as non-threatening but threatened. It served to magnify the hostility perceived by the republics in the central government.

On different occasions, the Russian leaders made statements picturing Russia as one of the republics, putting Russia on a par with other republics. There were several such statements. Once Yeltsin criticized Gorbachev for making negative remarks about Moldova and its struggle for independence. He added that Gorbachev's attitudes towards Moldova showed how he would react to Russia's independence.[14] After the armed attacks in Lithuania in January, 1991, Yeltsin said Russia might be the next target. In an effort to identify with the republics, Yeltsin told the Ukrainian parliament that Gorbachev was articulating ideas about the presidential form of government in the country without, most importantly, consulting with the republics.[15]

Russia tried to express and strengthen solidarity with the republics when the republics felt besieged by the centre. This was done primarily by appeals. After the Lithuanian incident in January, 1991, Yeltsin appealed to the Russian speaking population to remain calm and solve their problems through dialogue. He also appealed to the Russian soldiers stationed in the Baltic area not to shoot at civilians or act against the legally instituted governments in the republics. Along with the leaders of the Baltic republics Yeltsin signed an appeal to the UN Secretary General to call a conference on the Baltic republics.[16]

Russia's expression of solidarity with the republics helped it appear more flexible compared with the inflexible centre. It also made it easier for the republics to associate with Russia.

A new economic union

The work to lay the foundation for a new common market type of economic relations involved the republics as much as Russia. The republics, especially the Baltic republics, were active participants in an effort to create a common market in the Soviet Union.

In the treaties on bases of inter-state relations, provisions were inserted mandating the parties' cooperation in creating an economic union or a common Eurasian market. But even before such treaties of relations were signed, Russia was deeply involved in discussion and creation of common-market type ties.

The idea of the common market though might have come from the Baltic republics. In an effort to establish more open economic relations they probably suggested a common market. The Tallin conferences were the forums for discussions of such relations and also to negotiate about currencies and tariffs. There were five such conferences. All the five conferences were held in Tallin, Estonia.[17] These conferences were able to create a committee of heads of the republics to carry on consultations. The Tallin conferences provided for bilateral negotiations as well as multilateral negotiations. These conferences were to create an economic structure which appeared to be a parallel structure to the economic aspects of the union Gorbachev was trying to forge (Levitsky, August 6, 1990, p. 2).

The economic union was not going to be the only structure which would hold the republics together. Presumably the economic union was going to be the economic aspect of a different union that was also in the works.

An alternative union

It was in 1991 that Russia -- along with Belarus, Ukraine and Kazakhstan clearly started moving towards an alternative union. There was first mutual recognition of the actors as sovereign states then the process of establishing a different union commenced. After the Lithuanian crisis in January, 1991, Yeltsin declared in a news conference that he had met with the leaders of Belarus, Kazakhstan, and Ukraine, and they had talked about an alternative Union because things could not wait for a Union Treaty.[18] This was the different Union to which Yeltsin sometimes referred as the alternative Union and sometimes as the common position of the republics.

The agreement among Belarus, Russia, and Ukraine to coordinate price changes in the condition of market economy was viewed by the media as a step forward to a new union by these three republics (Tsikora, November 20, 1990, p. 1). It was interpreted as such because this was the first multilateral agreement aimed at economic unity. Later in February, Belarus, Kazakhstan, Russia, and Ukraine met. This meeting discussed a different Union treaty that these republics would offer and themselves sign. At this meeting, these important republics expressed their wish to create a different union, a union based on international law. In April, 1991, when the centre had already made concessions, Yeltsin told Russian deputies that if the centre went back on its word the republics would make up a different union.

The inter-republican cooperation of the Russian republic was not simply recognizing the republics as independent states but it also generated the Russian capability to lead the creation of a different union. It helped Russia to emerge as a credible rival to the Soviet government which could rely upon the important republics to cooperate in replacing an outmoded union.

Conclusion

This chapter has taken us through the different sets of cooperative actions Russia performed providing us with some insight into the overall purpose of this giant republic. Most of Russia's interactions could be grouped under the overall directions I discussed above. In addition to these, there were interactions which can be described as attempts to coordinate introduction of market relations, negotiation sessions, implementation efforts (for treaties already signed), consultation on expansion of relations, republic initiated actions. But speaking in general terms, Russia's cooperation was aimed at achieving the goals discussed above.

They show that Russia was not cooperating with the other republics to maintain the past economic relations, as some authors have assumed about inter-republican cooperation in general. As a matter of fact, even the explicitly economic treaties were not completely economic, for instance, Russia's economic treaty with Azerbaijan provided for the signing of treaties on a whole host of subjects, including culture. From the very beginning, Russia wanted to sign political treaties. Silaev once said that the political relations should be straightened out first. The more extensive and more important treaties were the treaties on the principles of inter-state relations. The economic treaties acted as evidence of Russia's goodwill as well as the mechanism that made the republics agree to sign the inter-state relations treaties. Thus the cooperative strategy of the RSFSR was multidimensional, not unidimensional. Russia did use a variety of activities, not just treaties, to put into effect a more liberal policy orientation as regards centre-periphery relations.

Through these legal instruments of treaties and protocols Russia was recognizing the republics' desire for independence thus becoming more forthcoming than the centre. The statements that Russian leaders made identifying with the republics and denouncing the centre also underlined Russia's support for the republic's aspirations. By being more lenient than the central government was willing to be, the Russian leaders were destroying the centre's ability to reconstruct the federation. By identifying with the republics it was reassuring them that it would not be like the centre and the republics should be afraid of the centre which was threatening everybody.

But at the same time, the treaties contained restrictive clauses like the ones on the minority issue which require the parties to cooperate on providing the minorities in each other's territories conditions for proper development. Russia's attempt to control the minority policies of the Baltic republics is another such attempt to restrict republican sovereignty. Thus Russia was willing to let go to a certain extent; it was more generous than the central government but not much more. The pattern of interactions also underscore that Russia was not an equal partner in the republican struggle to augment republican autonomy. The pattern clearly demonstrates that Russia, long before outside observers realized the USSR could not be maintained in the old form, wanted to reconstruct its relations in a more liberal direction. The general thrust of their inter-republican policy was to do that.

The fact that Russia had a calculated policy orientation does not mean that the whole process remained under Russian control all the time. The republics tried to exploit the more flexible Russian leadership, its dependence on the democrats in the Russian parliament, and the Russian elite's rivalry with the union government elite. An example is Armenia's Ter-Petrosyan's cabled message to Yeltsin. In this message he complained that Russian soldiers were stationed in Nagarno Karabakh and were used against Armenians by the Azerbaijanis. He also mentioned that Armenia was interested in concluding a long term treaty with Russia. The Lithuanians sometimes reminded Russia that Russian democracy could not survive if Lithuanian democracy was killed. There were many democrats in the Russian parliament who supported especially the Baltic republics' struggle, and Lithuania's reminders were aimed at generating pressures from these democrats on the Russian government. It was the democrats who held rallies in support of the Baltic republics' independence or to express solidarity with them.

The Baltic republics perhaps exercised some subtle pressure in the area of international cooperation. The case study deals with this in more

Flow of interactions 41

detail. One incident can be mentioned here. Russia and the Baltic republics went together to Sweden to discuss economic cooperation. The idea that they should meet Sweden together might have come from the Baltic republics. These republics probably suggested to Russia that they would help it, in any way they could, to establish external economic linkages. The case study in chapter five deals with such republican initiative.

Notes

1. For the letter written to the Lithuanian government see *Ekho Litvy* (July 11, 1990), 'Priglashenie k sotrudnichestvu', p. 1; for the letter written to Latvia see, *Izvestia* (July 11, 1990), 'Na peregovory s SSSR i RSFSR', p. 3.

2. *Bakinskii Rabochii* (September 4, 1990), 'Na osnove ravnopravia i vzaimnoi vuigody', p. 2.

3. *Ekho Litvy* (July 31, 1990), 'Soobshchenie o vstreche predsedatelei verkhovnykh sovetov Latviiskoi respubliki, Litovskoi respubliki, Rossiiskoi Sovetskoi Federativnoi Sotsialisticheskoi Respubliki i Estonoskoi respubliki', p. 1.

4. For the subjects dealt with by these treaties see *Kazakhstanskaya Pravda* (November 24, 1990), 'Text of Kazakh, RSFSR Cooperation Treaty', translated in *FBIS* (February 6, 1991), pp. 29-32.

5. On disagreement between Lithuania and Russia see *Ekho Litvy* (January 18, 1991), 'Gotovitsia dogovor s Rossiiskoi Federatsii', p. 2. On Latvia's withdrawal see *Baltiskoe Vremya* (October 23, 1990), 'Baltics RSFSR Official Comments on Latvia Talks', pp. 1-2; translated in *JPRS*, UPA 90, 071, 27.

6. For Lavtia's economic needs see, *TASS* (November 15, 1990), 'Latvia to Request Aid from Russia'; translated in *FBIS*, November 16, 1990, p. 59.

7. 'Ot chevo ukhodit i kuda idet Litva: beseda nashikh korrespondentov s primer ministrom respubliki Kazimeroi Prunskiene', op. cit.

8. For the treaty see *Ekho Litvy* (August 16, 1990), 'Peregovory mezhdu pravitelstvami Litvy i Rossiiskoi Federatsii', p. 1; for the agreement to sign a broader treaty see *Ekho Litvy* (August 17, 1990), 'Kommunique o

peregovorakh mezhdu pravitelstvami Rossiskoi Sovetskoi Sotsialisticheskoi Respubliki i Litovskoi Respubliki', p. 1.

9. For this statement see *Stockholm Svenska Dagbladet* (August 23, 1990), 'Russian Minister Sees Commonwealth Future', p. 8; translated in *FBIS* (August 29, 1990), pp. 69-70.

10. *Izvestia* (September 22, 1990), 'Predlozhenia i postanovlenia', p. 1.

11. For such interpretation of this resolution see *Radio Rossii Network* (January 13, 1991), 'Yeltsin Says Lithuania Next Afghanistan'; translated in *FBIS* (January 14, 1991), pp. 92-3.

12. For this protocol see *Vestnik Gruzii* (March 26, 1991), 'Joint RSFSR-Georgian Protocol Signed'; translated in *FBIS* (April 10, 1991), pp. 72-3.

13. *Izvestia* (November 14, 1990), 'Na sessii Verkhovnogo Soveta RSFSR: soyuznyi dogovor i suverenitet Rossii', p. 2.

14. *Izvestia* (September 26, 1990), 'Boris Yeltsin raziasniaet svaiu pozitsiu', p. 3.

15. *Izvestia* (November 20, 1990), 'Rossiya i Ukraina: ob"ediniayut usilia i resurci', p. 2.

16. For the appeal to the Russian speaking people see *Izvestia* (January 14, 1991), 'Tallin: Zayavlenie glav chiterikh respublik', p. 2; for the appeal to the Russian soldiers see, *FBIS* (January 14, 1991), pp. 92-3; for the joint appeal to the UN Secretary General see, *Ekho Litvy* (January 16, 1991), 'Obrashchenie k generalnomu sekretariu OON', p. 2.

17. For the five Tallin Conferences see *Ekho Litvy* (August 7, 1990), 'Soveshchanie v Talline', p. 3; *Ekho Litvy* (September 29, 1990), 'Tallinskoe soveshchanie: vtoroi round', p. 1; *Ekho Litvy* (December 11, 1990), 'Soobshchenie o iii Tallinskom soveshchanii', p. 1; *Ekho Litvy* (February 16, 1991), 'Soveshchanie v Talline', p. 1; *Ekho Litvy* (April 27, 1991), 'Vstrecha v Talline', p. 1.

18. *Rossiiskaya gazeta* (January 15, 1991), 'Press konferentsia predsedatelia Verkhovnogo Soveta RSFSR', p. 2.

4 Reciprocity in Unequal Relations: A Case Study of Lithuanian-Russian Cooperation

Introduction

Lithuania became the first Soviet republic to declare sovereignty or revive independence, as the Lithuanians themselves put it, on March 11, 1990.[1] From that day on, the Lithuanian government clung to the position that Lithuania would remain independent from the Soviet Union. Russia had the largest number of cooperative interactions with this republic. The Russian government at various times ardently supported Lithuania's position. In this chapter I study the relations between Lithuania and Russia during the period selected for the overall analysis. The next chapter examines the effect of Russia's policy on the centre's ability to tame Lithuania.

    Case studies serve different purposes, e.g., developing theories, testing models. They are used because comparative studies involving a number of cases must of necessity exclude many details so a certain degree of methodological rigor can be obtained. Case studies can capture most of the minute details essential for an adequate explanation. Indeed, case studies are used for precisely this reason -- to have all the details to make a construct subtler and a more nuanced explanation possible.[2]

    This book examines Russia's relations with fourteen other republics. Consequently, the methods used are keeping the analysis at the aggregate level since multiple case studies of Russia's relations with these fourteen republics are not feasible. To circumscribe the loss of details and to control for exclusion of potentially indispensable variables, I have conducted a case study of Lithuanian-Russian relations.

The case study does not simply present the global picture in a miniature, it also aims at rectifying some of the flaws generated by the use of the methods in the study. One such flaw is the absence of any scrutiny of the role of the republics. Thus far, the study almost gives the impression that the republics were passive instruments in the implementation of a Russian policy. Common sense would contradict such an assumption.

I have chosen Lithuania for a number of reasons. From all indications, Lithuania was used by the Russian government to signal its policy to other republics. Since Lithuania declared its independence first and remained fiercely nationalistic against the centre's overtures and pressures, Lithuanian-Russian relations represent a litmus test of Russian resolve in weakening the central government. These reasons aside, the Baltic states received generous media coverage because of Western attitudes on the incorporation of the Baltic republics in the Soviet Union and the nature of the Baltic nationalist movement. As a result, relatively more information is available on Lithuania.

I have divided the case study into two parts. In this chapter, I study the interactions between Lithuania and Russia, compare them with Lithuanian interactions with other republics, and look at the role Lithuania played in shaping the cooperative process. I also examine the role of the Russian democrats who played a part in this bilateral relations, and at the end study the pace at which the relations developed, i.e., if there had been any sudden changes in Lithuanian-Russian relations over the fourteen month period.

Russia's relations with Lithuania was the centrepiece of Russia's inter-republican policy. It demonstrated to all concerned how far Russia would go to support an intransigent republic, from the centre's standpoint, and a republic seeking freedom from the perspective of the republics. The Lithuanian-Russian relations set the tone for Russian policy.

The Russian government took shape at a time when Lithuania had already declared sovereignty and aroused the central government's ire. The central government had inflicted an economic blockade on this republic. The Lithuanian government was anxiously following events in Russia as well as busily devising strategies to neutralize the effects of the blockade and keep the fledgling state alive. It was at this juncture that the newly elected Russian leader, Boris Yeltsin, burst into the political scene with statements which clearly opposed the central government's position vis a vis Lithuania and the Baltic states in general.

Lithuanian-Russian relations

Russia demonstrated to Lithuania, other republics, and the centre that it did not approve of the centre's inexorable posture and would support Lithuania in its quest for sovereignty. Yeltsin condemned the economic blockade. Upon his election, Yeltsin said that one of the very first things he wanted to do was sign political and economic treaties with the Baltic republics. This made a Lithuanian observer remark, 'In fifty years, nobody holding such a high position uttered words Lithuania wanted to hear so much'.[3]

Many of Russia's actions were geared toward recognizing and helping to establish Lithuania's legal, sovereign existence. The Soviet central government persistently refused to recognize Lithuania formally as a separate state. Some of the actions of Russia clearly helped Lithuania maintain its firm stance against the central leadership.

Before the Treaty on the Bases of Inter-State Relations was signed with Lithuania on July 29, 1991, the Russian government recognized Lithuania in a protocol signed on August 17, 1990. When Lithuania acquired its own postage stamps Russia recognized them with the two parties signing a protocol on this in October, 1990. At a relatively early stage, an agreement signed by Russia and the Baltic republics in September, 1990, recognized the right of each republic to create and develop independent banking systems. All this was making the central government irksome. Russia's support remained consistent over time except for a significant break at the end of 1990. After the Soviet soldiers launched an armed attack against Lithuania in January 11-13, 1991, and the resulting capture by them of the Lithuanian radio and television tower, the Russian government came out very strongly in support of the Lithuanian government. It remained supportive till the August 1991 coup.

Immediately after the attack, Yeltsin, along with the three Baltic states, signed an appeal to the UN Secretary General to call a conference to solve the problems in the Baltic region (mainly Lithuania).[4] He denounced the use of force in a press conference -- at the same time appealing to the Russian soldiers deployed in the Baltic area not to interfere in the internal affairs of the republics. The Russian parliament came out with a declaration against military aggression in Lithuania.[5] The January incidents also led to two four-party declarations. In one of them Estonia, Latvia, Lithuania and Russia declared that they would aid one another in the event there was an attempt to overthrow any of their governments. In the other declaration, the same four pledged non-participation of their forces in a case of violation of any of their sovereignty.[6] Furthermore, Yeltsin wrote a lengthy letter to the people of Lithuania decrying the attack and identifying with the Lithuanians' struggle. Till the August 1991 coup the OMON of the MVD of the Soviet Union and Soviet soldiers engaged in almost continuous attacks against government buildings, banks, and border posts, and the Russian government staunchly supported the Lithuanian government; particularly an important demand of the Lithuanian leadership that the OMON troops should be withdrawn from Lithuanian territory. The effort to help Lithuania be established as a sovereign state culminated in signing the treaty on inter-state relations in July 1991.

Equally important as the recognition of Lithuania as an independent state was assisting it to become viable as a state economically. Soon after the Russian parliamentary elections, Vytautas Landsbergis, chair of the Lithuanian parliament, met Yeltsin. It was made clear that Russia was interested in signing treaties with Lithuania and other republics. The economic blockade of the central government was wreaking havoc on the Lithuanian economy and the Lithuanian government was desperately trying to shore up the economy by seeking linkages with republics, regions and enterprises. Because of the blockade prices in general rose. Fuel prices shot up causing inflation. Consequently, social problems were intensifying. Lithuania needed petroleum, metals, and lumber.[7] The RSFSR and Lithuania quickly negotiated and signed an economic treaty on August 16, 1990. This treaty was signed to maintain 1990 level of supply of goods between the two republics in 1991. The treaty was viewed by observers as Russia extending a helping hand to bolster Lithuania's position against the centre.

The RSFSR government was keen on developing a common market structure in the USSR. It would serve as an alternative to the present centrally controlled economic relations. It is true that the first Tallin meeting was called at Estonian initiative but Russia simply did not respond to Estonia's proposals. Alexander Granberg, head of the RSFSR parliamentary committee on Inter-republican Relations, Regional Politics and Cooperation, went to visit Lithuania to sound out the Lithuanian leadership on a common market. During the visit he said he had been advocating such relations but many in the central government did not appreciate the ideas.

With Lithuania, just as with other republics, it was not simply helping to establish an infant state as a sovereign member of the world community and in the process undercutting the union government authority and legitimacy but also signing an inter-state relations treaty which established very close relations with Lithuania. A treaty on Kaliningrad was also signed in which Lithuania accepted Kaliningrad as a part of Russia and agreed to work together with the Kaliningrad local administration so it could be sustained and developed as a region of Russia. The foregoing chapter has already discussed some other Russian actions which were clearly limiting Lithuania's sovereignty. The Kaliningrad agreement substituted Russian authority for that of the centre and Lithuania, which on occasions claimed this territory accepted Russian claim.

Lithuania and the Other Republics

Lithuania was not only interacting with Russia; it had a policy of developing good relations with all the republics of the Soviet Union and the regions thereof. Lithuania's relations with the other two Baltic republics were close though sometimes they seemed to be struggling to maintain a consensus about the central government. On the whole, the Baltic republics were on the same side in a war and acting as comrades in arms. In this section I try to find out if Lithuania's relations with the non-Baltic republics differ in a significant manner from its relations with Russia. One of the arguments I posit in the study is, the Russian elites were in many ways behaving like an imperial elite, i.e., they were trying to protect Russian interests as best they could in a changed environment through linkages in all spheres of life. Lithuania's relations with other non-Baltic republics could give added support to that assumption. I have selected written agreements rather than visits or supportive statements or actions of the sort. As far as non-written cooperative actions are concerned, there were not that many. There was a Georgian club established to disseminate information on Lithuania, Ukraine once supplied fuel to Lithuania during the blockade and a Ukrainian doctors' team came on a visit, and a Lithuanian delegation went to Georgia to help establish contact between the government and the South Ossetians, but other than such activities the non-written interactions were not all that significant. For instance, the Ukrainian government did not demand any special program implemented for the Ukrainians, or the Belarusian government for the Belarusians for that matter. The chief goal of this analysis is to discover if it was a tendency of the Lithuanian government to sign wide-ranging cooperation treaties with republics other than the Baltic republics and Russia, treaties that established as close and multi-dimensional a relationship as the one established by the inter-state relations treaty signed with Russia.

Available information on Lithuania's agreements with other republics cannot help draw definitive conclusions but they are suggestive and some tentative conclusions can be derived. The agreements that Lithuania proposed to other republics and signed were of limited nature. Except the agreement signed with Armenia in August 1991 for which special reasons existed, Lithuania evinced a tendency not to sign or propose treaties of as broad a scope as the one it signed with Russia although it had a clear, declared policy of nurturing intimate ties with the republics of the Soviet Union.

A Lithuanian delegation came to Azerbaijan in September 1990 to discuss bilateral cooperation. It foresaw signing an agreement on economic, scientific and technical cooperation, in other words economic cooperation. A treaty on trade, economic, scientific-technical and economic issues was signed between Lithuania and Tadjikistan, a republic which wanted to remain within the Union, in September, 1990. During the signing of this treaty, both sides emphasized the economic nature of the agreement. Similar agreements with scientific-technical-economic contents were signed with Kyrgyzia, Moldova, and Ukraine in late 1990. The Lithuanian government signed two more agreements with Ukraine in the first half of 1991. One of them was a protocol on the implementation of the earlier economic treaty, the other was a purely cultural agreement on educational, scientific cooperation and student exchange. Kiev and Vilnius became sister cities in June 1991. The chief reason for this, as one initiator of the move put it, was to facilitate the free cultural development of the Ukrainians living in Vilnius and Lithuanians living in Kiev.

The treaty of general inter-state cooperation with Armenia signed in August, 1991, constitutes the sole exception to Lithuania's pattern of signing treaties of limited, specific contents with non-Russian, non-Baltic republics. This treaty was signed later than the treaty signed with Russia. The treaty was signed for important reasons. Armenia and Lithuania were both republics that had expressed unwillingness to sign the Union Treaty. Along with the four other republics averse to signing the treaty, they were feeling insecure fearing punitive measures from the central government. Their status seemed uncertain at best. As Ter-Petrosyan said, these two republics had identical future problems.[8]

The Lithuanian government's written agreements with non-Russian and non-Baltic republics were of either economic or cultural substance. This points at two facts about Lithuania's interactions with these republics: first, Lithuania was not interested in strong, extensive ties; second, the other republics did not ask for such relations as well.

Lithuania's role

The part played by Lithuania in the Lithuanian-Russian cooperative relationship is the classic example of the creative struggle for independence waged by a small, dominated state. The Lithuanian-Russian interactions did not only signify a strategy on Russia's part but also aggressive courtship of the Russian government by the Lithuanian leaders. The more important aspects of the Lithuanian role are dealt with in the next chapter; here I touch upon some of the less subtle manoeuvres.

The Sajudis leaders in power at the time were not passive tools in the hands of the Russian legislative leaders to be used to increase the influence of the Russian elites against the Union government. They were active participants in the process. They diligently sought assistance from the Russian government and performed their part in helping out the Russian leadership. The Russian leaders understood they could rely on the Lithuanians.

The democrats of Russia, individually and in the form of the movement Democratic Russia were the mainstay in the support base of Yeltsin and his close associates. The Lithuanian government considered Yeltsin a major figure in the Union-wide democratic movement. They reached out to the democrats in the Russian government at the republic level as well as the local level. There were divisions, as the next chapter documents, in the Lithuanian government on its Russia policy but the policy itself reflected the bend of the pro-Russia elements in the Lithuanian government.

The Lithuanian leaders tried to win Russian empathy and retain it. From a very early period, Lithuanian leaders started keeping an eye on developments in Russia. During his press conference in Prague, Landsbergis was asked if he thought Yeltsin's election as the chair of the Russian parliament would affect things, he replied 'Yes' adding that Yeltsin's name was associated with the democratic movement. Landsbergis was one of the first, if not the first, republican leader to meet Yeltsin after Yeltsin became chairman of the Russian legislature. Lithuanian political observers noted that Yeltsin would tear down the economic blockade from the other side.

As part of its strategy to woo Russian leaders, Lithuania made some symbolic and, by and large, token gestures. It published Yeltsin's biography. The Ministry of Culture decided to show the lengthy documentary film on Yeltsin made in the Sverdlovsk film studio. The Lithuanians invited the democrats in the Russian parliament to attend the celebration of the 70th anniversary of the Lithuanian-Russian treaty in July 1990. Through this treaty Russia had recognized the independence of Lithuania. During the solemn session of celebration, Landsbergis paid tribute to the Russian democrats who had supported Lithuanian independence before 1920.

Landsbergis and other Lithuanian leaders tried strenuously to relate Lithuania's independence to the movement for democracy in Russia and elsewhere in the USSR. Particularly Landsbergis compared Russia's emergence with a step toward creating democracy. To identify with the democratic forces Lithuania attended in April, 1991, the first inter-parliament conference of the republics of the USSR which, among other things, supported the coal-mine strikes.

Lithuania had a deliberate policy of collaborating with the radical democratic forces in Russia. To do that, it made concrete efforts involving tangible resources. An art gallery named 'Bakshto' opened in Vilnius with the specific purpose to display works of young artists. One of its goals was to have exhibitions of works done by young Leningrad and Moscow artists, works with which Lithuanians were not familiar. Moscow and Leningrad were two cities which supplied most Russian democrats and had democrat-dominated city governments at the time. Lithuania also named a street in Central Vilnius after Andrei Sakharov. Sakharov's widow, Yelena Bonner, herself a prominent democrat, came to the dedication ceremony at which she said that Lithuania would be free because she was right. She also praised its peaceful, non-violent struggle.

'People's Diplomacy' was a method used by the Lithuanian government to shore up the support base of the Russian government as well as create a reservoir of good will and sympathy in Russia for the Lithuanians. People's Diplomacy originated as a concept from a session of the Assembly (Sejm) of the Sajudis. It was a suggestion to cultivate relations with different regions of the USSR. Later, in practice, it also amounted to strengthening ties at the citizens' levels. The Lithuanian government encouraged it and participated in it. When the coal miners' strike was going on in Russia and Ukraine in Spring 1991, the Lithuanian Workers' Union mounted a major campaign to collect foods for the striking coal miners. They collected 500 tons of foods for the miners. Again in July the Lithuanian Workers' Union invited the children of the coal miners from Kuzbass to vacation in Lithuania. Half the cost of the vacation was borne directly by the Lithuanian government (Sripov, July 2, 1991, p. 2). It is not a coincidence that the coal miners of Russia demanded Gorbachev's and the USSR government's resignation and later the dissolution of the Union parliament. Furthermore, they supported Yeltsin. The coal miners, as a matter of fact, were an island of opposition to the CPSU among the largely supportive or indifferent working class of Russia.[9]

In its cooperation with the Russian government, Lithuania initiated interactions on a number of occasions. The Lithuanian Supreme Council appealed for support to the Supreme Soviet of the RSFSR and the people of Russia in which it stressed the bond of friendship between the Lithuanian and Russian peoples. When the Russian conservative forces seemed to be gaining an upper hand in the parliament in early 1991, the Presidium of the Supreme Council of Lithuania sent a telegram to the Russian Supreme Soviet and its

Chairman. The telegram informed that the Lithuanian government was watching the session very carefully and wished them well. It reminded that preservation of democracy, development of opposition to dictatorship and real economic and political perestroika depended on self-determination of Russia.

Prime Minister G. Vagnarius's telegram to the government of Russia in May, 1991, identified the security of the Lithuanian government with that of the Russian government. It highlighted the link between Russian democracy and security of other republics. He sent this telegram requesting help from the Russian government against the attacks by the OMON troops and the MVD soldiers on Lithuanian border guards. Vagnarius stressed that attacks against Lithuania would translate into action against Moscow (Russia).

In a spirit of hanging in together, Vagnarius also sent a telegram congratulating Silaev upon his selection as the prime minister of Russia. Lithuania and the other two Baltic republics adopted an appeal to the Supreme Soviet of the Russian republic to develop relations on the basis of the peace treaty of 1920 that was signed between Lithuania and Russia thus suggesting the kind of relations they desired.

Some financial losses were endured by Lithuania to keep supplies to Russia flowing. When the Russian Prime Minister was alarmed that 50% cut in the state subsidies by the Lithuanian government on meat products, milk and bread, were going to raise their prices, premier Vagnarius responded that Lithuania would not do anything that would harm the Russian economy. As a matter of fact, he noted, Lithuania's budget had to cover some costs of supplying goods to Russia at low prices. The items would be supplied at fixed prices -- he assured.[10]

The new leaders of Lithuania tried to make the Russian government understand what an asset Lithuania would be to the rest of the Soviet Union. This was not a reward dangled in front of only the Russian leadership but also to the Russian people and specific political forces to make Lithuanian independence more palatable. The Sajudis leadership wanted to make Lithuania a link between the East and the West. Lithuania would be the window to the West for the eastern part of Europe. This really meant that it was going to be easy for Lithuania to attract foreign capital and foreign technology by virtue of its status as a western country and the level of its development. Russia could get in touch with western businesses through Lithuania. Lithuania could help Russia establish economic and business contacts. The whole Baltic region seemed to have adopted such a position. Russia did go to Sweden once with the Baltic states to negotiate for economic aid. Lithuania herself arranged seminars in which Western and Russian representatives participated.

One of the theses orienting this study is the Russian elites were deliberately trying to safeguard imperial interests. Such an argument tends to marginalize the republics as mere ploys in Russian hands to be used against the centre. But in Lithuania's case, that is far from the truth. Lithuania was not passively letting itself be used. On the contrary, it was an active participant and was sometimes trying to manipulate Russia.

In addition to direct government actions, there must have been some indirect manoeuvres by the Lithuanian government. Some publication trends in the Lithuanian press, especially the major newspaper *Ekho Litvy* betray government influence. *Ekho Litvy*, towards the end of 1990, published a series of articles on Lithuanian Russian time-tested friendship at different levels including popular and intellectual.[11]

The democrats in Lithuanian-Russian relations

The democrats and democracy in Russia and the whole Union itself were recurrent themes in the speeches and remarks of Lithuanian leaders whenever they touched upon Lithuanian-Russian relations. They said Lithuania was watching closely the development of Russian democracy because it would have an important bearing on Lithuania's fate. They thought the centre wanted to kill off Lithuanian independence because the democrats in other republics looked up to Lithuania. The conclusion was that Lithuania's fate would be determined by how much support it could get and maintain from the democratic forces first in Russia and then throughout the whole Soviet Union. The Russian democrats for their part came to Lithuania and thanked it for serving as an example of democracy and freedom.

One of the components, it should be recalled, of the principal argument of this book is that the Russian democrats were part of the coalition supporting the Yeltsin government in Russia. Within Russia itself the democratic movement was class based and its members came from the intelligentsia (Clarke, 1992). Many of them started focusing on Russia and Yeltsin after losing faith in Gorbachev. They understood, long before Gorbachev did, that the CPSU could not be democratized. Democratic Russia emerged as a structure embodying the goals of the more radical democrats who wanted an end to the rule of the CPSU. The democrats wanted to liberalize state society relations, and democratize politics in the USSR. The most radical ones considered the Bolshevik revolution itself a mistake (Clarke, 1992). Among the most important democrats were: A. Sobchak, the Mayor of Leningrad; G. Popov the Mayor of Moscow, Yu. Afanasyev, the historian, E. Kliamkin, the scholar.

Both inside and outside the Russian parliament the democrats were a strong source of support for Yeltsin and his policies. Democratic Russia offered its unstinting support to Yeltsin in his bid for the Russian presidency and worked for his victory during the election campaign (Urban, 1992). The democrats of Russia saw Lithuania's survival as a state as part of their struggle to democratize the USSR by undermining the CPSU's rule in the periphery and by generating support for the alternative of Yeltsin government and for the reformers-democrats ruled localities. This is not to say that all democrats equally supported republican independence.[12] Since the democrats formed the strongest supporting pillar for the Yeltsin government their role in promoting Lithuanian-Russian cooperative relations and their support for Lithuania's sovereignty deserve consideration. They supported Lithuania in its uphill struggle to gain and maintain sovereignty. The extent of support offered to Lithuania points at one conclusion and that is the democrats had an important role in fashioning Russian policy towards Lithuania. Their sympathy for the Lithuanian government impetuously expressed on various occasions kept the pressure on the Russian governing elite. Not only that, they also worked in concert with the Russian government in their empathy for Lithuania.

Grass roots activities were organized to oppose the central government's actions in Lithuania and the whole Baltic region. The purpose of these pickets was to display solidarity with the Lithuanians and portray them as the aggrieved party. The two more important grassroots actions were organized in Ivanovo and Sverdlovsk. In Ivanovo, picket participants organized an anti-blockade fund and held placards saying 'The Nazis blockaded Leningrad, CPSU Lithuania', and 'Lithuania is independent, not Soviet'. The residents of Sverdlovsk collected signatures to a statement declaring they recognized the statehood of Lithuania and opposed sanctions against it. This document also supported the breakup of the Soviet 'empire'. There were visits from the democratic elements in the cultural world of Leningrad.[13] The democratic movements of Russia, Ukraine and some other republics sent a group of young people to Lithuania, in a gesture of unity, to defend the Lithuanian parliament against military aggression in early 1991.

At the elite and organizational levels, the democratic forces recognized Lithuania and accepted it as an independent state, collaborated with it to strengthen the union-wide democratic movement, aided it to expose the Union government as the culprit, and condemned the attacks in January, 1991, against Lithuania. The democrats' unequivocal acceptance of Lithuanian statehood and recognition of it were expressed in various ways. One of them was the goodwill mission in June 1990 of about 100 delegates of the democratic movements of Russia. They were deputies of the Moscow Soviet, the Leningrad Soviet and the law-making bodies of other areas. They endorsed the craving of the Lithuanian people to be independent and denounced the president of the USSR. In their press conference they declared that Lithuania and Russia should become friendly states, considerably down playing conflicts between ethnic Russians and Lithuanians inside Lithuania. Whenever the Lithuanian government celebrated Lithuania's statehood or its independence, it almost always extended invitations to prominent Russian democratic figures. When the Lithuanian legislature celebrated the anniversary of the 1920 treaty with Russia which recognized Lithuania as a sovereign state, deputies from the Leningrad Soviet, Moscow Soviet, Cheliabinsk Soviet, and Orlov Soviet came to attend. The Lithuanian Supreme Council session held after the Lithuanian referendum in which the population had opted for independence was attended by representatives of the Russian Democratic Union along with those of the Russian foreign ministry.[14]

The informal group Memorial both recognized Lithuanian statehood and urged the Union government to accept it as a sovereign state when it passed the resolution disapproving use of economic sanctions and use of coercion against the Baltic states. The resolution asked the Soviet government to negotiate with the Baltic states recognizing the declaration of revival of statehood by them. Despite its support for the Baltic states, Memorial apparently had mixed feelings. The resolution did make the point that the Baltic situation was precarious because it might lead to the negation of *perestroika* by the conservative forces.[15] This demonstrates that support from the democratic camp was not unadulterated; there also lurked the fear that the Baltic states might spoil everything.

At least one element in the Russian democratic movement tried to help Lithuania expose the Union government as the perpetrators of the crimes against Lithuania. The group 'Shchit', whose leader was a deputy in the RSFSR Supreme Soviet, came to investigate the military attacks on Lithuania in January 11-13, 1991. They concluded that the January events were a coup attempt orchestrated by the Communist Party of Lithuania and Gorbachev was aware of it. The members of Shchit believed that if democracy triumphed in Lithuania it would benefit not only Lithuania and Russia but the people of the whole Union.

The January 1991 armed attacks against Lithuania were a turning point in official Lithuanian-Russian relations as well as relations between Lithuania and democratic forces in Russia. There was a lapse in democratic and Russian government support for Lithuania at the end of 1990 and which I discuss later in this chapter. After the January aggression both the democrats and the Russian government were jolted into action. Repentant democrats streamed into Lithuania to atone for the sin. They stressed that the democratic movement was uncoordinated, the system was beyond reform (Sheinberg, February 2, 1991, p. 2). It was after January that at least three major gatherings of democratic forces were held to enhance collaboration among themselves. The first was the Congress of Democratic Forces held in Kharkov; the principal item on the agenda was the Baltic states. The second was a mammoth gathering in support of the democratic forces in Russia organized by Sajudis, Democratic Party of Labour of Lithuania and other Lithuanian political parties. Guests from Belarus, Russia, and Ukraine participated. The meeting was used to denounce red terror, Gorbachev, and the Union Treaty. The Lithuanians thanked the Russian representatives for their support. The Belarusians, Russians, Ukrainians, in turn, thanked Lithuania for lessons in democracy and help (Osherov, March 19, 1991, p. 2). In April, the first inter-parliament conference of the republics was held. Aside from supporting the striking coal miners, it declared that it was necessary to work jointly with workers to bring about radical changes to ensure the real sovereignty of the republics.

Lithuanian government leaders, members of parliament, opposition party leaders, political observers and even common citizens understood and stressed the link between Lithuanian independence and the Russian democratic forces. The government, we have noticed, tried to link Lithuania's independence with the Russian democratic movement. At different times government leaders acknowledged that the Russian democratic movement helped and would help Lithuania retain its independence. The deputy chairman of the Supreme Council of Lithuania, B. Kuzmitskas said at the solemn session of the legislature celebrating the treaty between Lithuania and Russia signed in 1920 that both the Union-wide democratic movement and the Russian democratic movement would assist Lithuania retain its sovereignty. N. Medvedev, a member of the Lithuanian parliament stressed the need to work in collaboration with other democrats to neutralize Soviet soldiers so they could not be used against civilians.

The democrats did not only support Lithuania but also the other two Baltic republics and the other two Baltic republics were for stronger ties with the Russian democrats.[16] Many in the Russian democratic movement were inclined to let the republics be independent.

The unofficial ties between the Russian democrats and the Lithuanian government and the democrats' official ties with the Russian government led by Boris Yeltsin suggest that there must have been substantial democratic input into the Russian government's decision to cooperate with the republics, certainly the Baltic republics, and particularly Lithuania. Democratic Russia openly advocated republican independence as an element in its own agenda (Wishnevsky, 1992, pp. 23-7). This is why from time to time the Lithuanian government reminded the Russian leaders how important Lithuania's survival was for Russia. Evidently, the Lithuanian government was trying to create pressure on the Russian elites.

A not so abrupt break

The cooperative interactions between Lithuania and Russia did not develop at an even pace although the beginning was enthusiastic on both the actors' parts. The pattern of relations between them reveals a break in 1990 which supports the major assumption of this study -- that the RSFSR wanted to weaken the USSR government -- and merits close attention.

At the end of 1990, Lithuania and Russia had hardly any bilateral interaction in the spirit demonstrated soon after the formation of the Russian government. This spirit reappeared after Lithuania suffered the January attacks. Both official and unofficial Russian interactions virtually stopped in this period.

The period October 1990-early January 1991 can be labelled a period of almost total estrangement of Lithuania from Russia. This break in cooperation coincided with the rapprochement between Gorbachev and the Russian government. The Lithuanian government officials started to sense elements of uncertainty being introduced from early August 1990 onward when K. Prunskiene noticed that the Russian Council of Ministers were drawing up the reform plan to be used for the whole Union. They took special note when Gorbachev and Yeltsin agreed on the formation of a working group to work out a programme for the whole Union on transition to a market economy. The group was to work under both Gorbachev and Yeltsin's authority. The Lithuanian government was clearly unnerved by the emergence of an apparently unified position between Gorbachev and the Russian Republic leadership. They felt the need to heighten horizontal relations with other republics, individual enterprises. By early October 1990, they found their room for manoeuvre progressively shrinking.[17]

In November 1990, Gorbachev and Yeltsin met with the results widely perceived as entailing concessions by Gorbachev to the Russian leader. They agreed that a number of joint USSR-RSFSR committees would be formed to hammer out bases from which a unified position could emerge to form the foundation of the union treaty. Right after this meeting, Yeltsin, appearing before the Russian Constitutional Commission, declared 'We are for a strong Union of Soviet Socialist Republics'.[18] It was immediately after this meeting between Gorbachev and Yeltsin that Prunskiene had an icy reception from the Russian vice premier Yavlinsky and was nearly rebuffed by G. Popov, a paramount figure in the Russian democratic movement and an erstwhile ally of Lithuania. Popov told her that Lithuania must operate its economic policy within ever narrower limits because the centre had got back its previous authority from Russia. Upon her return from Moscow, she described the encounters as the burning of bridges.

Lithuania's separation from the Russian elites exemplified by lack of active government and non-government support was starkly visible. This period saw almost no bilateral interactions between them although there were many occasions when Russian support or presence of Russian representatives were automatic in the past and would be after January 1991. There were hardly any contacts between the Lithuanian government and Russian democrats despite the fact that the Lithuanians needed their support. The message got through to the Lithuanian government leaders and it did not try to initiate contacts with its Russian counterpart. One thing that stood out as a glaring evidence of interruption in Lithuanian-Russian relations was the failure of Lithuanian leaders to mention the support lent by the Russian government and the Russian democrats to the Lithuanian independence struggle in any major speech. In the past the speeches of important Lithuanian government leaders came sprinkled with generous praise for the Russian democrats and the Russian leadership for standing beside the Lithuanians in their time of need.

This period itself was one of the hardest times the just revived Lithuanian state had been through, a time when it needed active support from its allies, yet none came from Russia. This was the time when the Lithuanian government felt the threat from the centre growing. It seemed to them that the centre was closing in on Lithuania. The Lithuanian leaders felt the centre would use force against Lithuania. In November, 1990, the USSR Supreme Soviet passed a resolution giving the USSR President the power to use any means to keep order in the society. It alarmed the Lithuanian government which thought the union government was about to force it to sign the Union Treaty. It accused the Gorbachev government of having an alternative, loyal to the centre, Lithuanian puppet government on hand to place it in Lithuania after the legitimate Lithuanian government was toppled. The Union Defence Minister Dmitri Yazov asked the Soviet soldiers stationed in Lithuania to stop actions aimed at besmirching the Union, destruction of Soviet monuments and to closely watch the Lithuanian press. At one point, Vice Premier R. Ozolas and Landsbergis were talking about defending Lithuania with arms and a creeping right wing dictatorship in the Soviet Union. Landsbergis visited both Great Britain and the US seeking support against the central government's impending military action against his government, but to no avail. For Lithuania this time was fraught with dangers but it could not go and ask for support from the Russian government.

It was under these circumstances that the Baltic council called a joint session of the legislatures of the three Baltic republics to figure out how to act, and to deflect pressure. A principal aim of the meeting, held in December, 1990, was to draw the world's attention to the Baltic region. Representatives of the legislatures of Armenia, Georgia, Moldova, and Ukraine came. None came from the Russian Supreme Soviet. One democrat from the Leningrad gorsoviet showed up. S. Berezenski, a member of Democratic Russia and the Leningrad Soviet, came only to observe not to show solidarity as did the Armenians or Ukrainians. His statements, in marked contrast to previous statements made by Russian democrats while visiting Lithuania, lacked support or enthusiasm. He said, for instance, that the Baltic states left the Union hastily; had they remained they would have been able to influence events from within.

It is true that the Russian government, Yeltsin, Silaev, or Yavlinsky, was not actively supporting Lithuania at the time, nonetheless, they did not renounce their inter-republican cooperation policy. It was a time when Gorbachev, in a last ditch attempt, yielded to the Russian government and had it involved in an effort to get the USSR out of the political and economic crisis. Lithuania was a major irritant to the central government because it did not want to be even in the renewed Union, and the central leaders rightly felt it was radicalizing the Baltic situation. Apparently one of the compromises the Russian government made was to significantly tone down its strident support for this Baltic state. The democrats' alliance with the Russian government steered them to the same choice. Some democrats themselves felt they needed to support Gorbachev in his attempt to pull the country out of the crisis.[19]

Conclusion

Overall, Russia had a large number of cooperative interactions with Lithuania. Its official interactions confirm the broad pattern of Russia's cooperative actions with other republics. Russia, unlike the centre, was ready to accept Lithuania as an independent state. Its economic treaty signed before the broad-based inter-state relations treaty had the aim of propping up the new government against the centre and got Russia the Lithuanian consent for broadening relations with Russia. Russia recognized, supported, and defended Lithuania after attacks in January by Union soldiers. This combination of support for the Lithuanian statehood and reestablishment of intimate ties form the core of my argument -- Russia clearly supported Lithuania's claim against the centre's vision of the future reconstituted Soviet state thus corroding the central government's legitimacy as the predominant actor in the struggle for the redefinition of centre-periphery relations.

Lithuania's agreements with other republics reveal a pattern. The leaders of Lithuania evinced a desire to sign agreements of limited scopes. They preferred not to sign agreements of as wide a range as that they signed with Russia. This suggests that Lithuania had reluctance to enter into wide-ranging agreements and probably felt obliged to sign the treaty with Russia which covered every aspect of its life as a state.

The case study does unearth information about one important factor. This is the relation of Russian democrats to the whole process. Russian democrats were fleetingly mentioned in the second chapter at the construction of my argument. The democratic factor has been present in the argument of the study as a shadow, never taking on the importance that the case study lends it. Many democrats of Russia supported as a general policy independence of the republics because that was the republics' demands and also because they thought it would further enervate CPSU rule. Their support for the Baltic republics were more intense because these republics were under the control of non-CPSU movements. By offering independence to the republics the democrats hoped to enlist their support for their agenda or the alternative future they envisaged for the Soviet Union. At least from Lithuania, they had different kinds of supports including morale boosts. But whether the democrats were as active in supporting the non-Baltic republics remains an open question.

The relatively short interruption in Lithuanian-Russian cooperation lends weight to the argument that Russia's inter-republican cooperation aimed at eliminating the central government as a strong contender on the political scene of the Soviet union. It is important to keep in mind that Russia and the Russian democrats virtually stopped giving active support to Lithuania and stopped encouraging it when Gorbachev accepted the Russian elites as partners in remaking the Union and yielded much to the Russian government. Gorbachev and Yeltsin were talking about a coalition government in the centre. Clearly, the Russians acceded to the demands of the central government not to encourage Lithuania which was bent on staying out of the Union. The Russian government and its democratic allies accepted the control over policy that Gorbachev offered rather than let conservative elements in the Union government gain further influence.

But the tactical moves on parts of both Gorbachev and the Russian elites unravelled after the January 1991 armed aggression committed against Latvia and Lithuania. The Russian government saw in it the increasing dominance of unreconstructed hard line communists. Its atonement for the partial abandonment of the Lithuanian allies was expressed through ever stronger condemnation of the attacks and continued cooperation thereafter. Russian democrats, in their turn, renewed interactions and regretted the uncoordinated nature of their movement, and admitted the need to build a unified democratic movement.

Lithuania tried to use the elite conflict to its advantage and wanted to benefit from the impetus for democratization. Its role is indicative of the part the republics played in Russia's inter-republican politics. The Lithuanian leaders readily offered themselves as allies to the Russians and declared themselves fellow soldiers in a struggle for democracy. At times they played on the fears of the Russian democrats drawing attention to the fact that if Lithuania was crushed it would be a significant loss for the democrats. By declaring alliance with the Russians they made the Russians confident about the success of their inter-republican policy. But these were some of the more explicit ways that Lithuania involved itself in Russia's inter-republican cooperation. The next chapter deals with the subtler and more creative tactics.

This part of the case study has examined the nature of Lithuanian-Russian relations, involvement of the democrats, the pace of cooperation and how they affect the major argument. But what of the impact of Lithuanian-Russian relations on Lithuanian-USSR relations? Assuming Russia desired to weaken the central government in the context of centre-periphery relations, how did the republics take advantage of this orientation of Russia? The next chapter addresses these questions.

Notes

1. Research for this chapter was done mainly using the Lithuanian daily *Ekho Litvy*. For citations for any specific information see Begum, Anwara (1995), *Inter-Republican Cooperation of the Russian Republic*, Ph.D. Dissertation, The University of Arizona, Tucson, Arizona, chapter, 4; or contact the author.

2. On the utility of case studies see Eckstein, Harry (1975), 'Case Study and Theory in Political Science' in Greenstein, Fred., and Polsby, Nelson (eds), *Handbook of Political Science*, vol. 7, Addison-Wesley, Reading,

Massachusetts. Also see Gibbs, David (1991), *The Political Economy of Third World intervention: Mines, Money, and US Policy in the Congo Crisis*, University of Chicago Press, Chicago.

3. For the statement see *Ekho Litvy* (June 6, 1990), 'Daidzhest pressa Litvy', p. 3.

4. For the appeal see *Ekho Litvy* (January 16, 1991), 'Obrashchenie k generalnomu sekretariu OON', p. 2.

5. For the declaration see *Moscow News* (January 20-26, 1991), 'Yeltsin Fears Major Onslaught on Democracy', no. 3; published in *FBIS* (February 11, 1991), p. 90.

6. For these two declarations see the following two reports in *Ekho Litvy* (February 19, 1991), 'Torzhestvennoe zacedanie', p. 1; and (January 16, 1991), 'Zayavlenie', p. 2.

7. On the Lithuanian economic problems resulting from the blockade many newspaper reports are available. Of them see, *Ekho Litvy* (June 7, 1990), 'Kommunike Litovskogo pravitel'stva', pp. 1, 2.

8. See *Ekho Litvy* (August 16, 1991), 'U nas est' obshchi problemy i obshchi zaboty', p. 1.

9. Sending humanitarian aid to the striking coal miners was not a peculiarly Lithuanian initiative to strengthen support for the Russian government. At least one more Baltic republic did the same. The Latvian Supreme Council instructed the cabinet to organize a similar effort in Latvia. See *Ekho Litvy* (March 15, 1991), 'Riga', under Puls Planety, p. 4. About the Russian working class and CPSU in the period see, Clarke, Terry (1992), *The Collapse of the Soviet Union: A Study of Demokratizatsia*, Ph.D. thesis, University of Illinois, Urbana-Champaign.

10. For Vagnarius's response see *Ekho Litvy* (July 9, 1991), 'Telegrama I. Silaevu', p. 1.

11. Here are two typical pieces, *Ekho Litvy* (November 15, 1990), 'Podderzhka is Rossii', pp. 4,5; *Ekho Litvy* (February 19, 1991), 'S chego nachinaetsia rodina', p. 2.

12. For Vitaly Korotich's opposition see, *Ekho Litvy* (November 17, 1990), 'Sevodnia Rossiya vozvrashchaetsia v chelaviechestvo', p. 2.

13. For instance, the visit of a theatre group to Vilnius. The director boasted of the group's democratic and unofficial character. See, *Ekho Litvy* (September 5, 1990), 'Vpervie v Litve', p. 4.

14. *Ekho Litvy* (February 2, 1991), 'Na sessii Verkhovnogo Sovieta respubliki', p. 1. It should be noted that the Democratic Union was one of the most radical democratic parties in Russia, see Orttung, Robert (1992), *Democratization in Leningrad*, Ph.D. thesis, University of California, Los Angeles.

15. For this resolution see *Ekho Litvy* (June 13, 1990), 'Resoliutsiya Memoriala', p. 2.

16. See *Ekho Litvy* (March 15, 1991), 'Riga', under Puls Planety, p. 4. According to this report, the Supreme Council of Latvia asked the cabinet to work with community and workers' organizations to send humanitarian aid to striking coal miners. It also suggested that a session of the Baltic Council be called to discuss the issue of cooperation with the democratic forces in Russia. Also see 'Leningrad', under Soobshchaet SIA in the same issue of the newspaper. This is a report on A. Sobchak, the mayor of Leningrad and an important democrat promising to cooperate with Estonia not withstanding the attitudes of the central government.

17. On the Lithuanian government's reactions and feeling of uncertainty after the formation of the Working Group see the following reports, all published in *Ekho Litvy* (August 10, 1990), 'Predposilki dal'neishikh otnoshenii Litovskoi respubliki s SSSR i RSFSR', p. 1; (August 11, 1990), 'Vstrecha ministrov', p. 3; (September 21, 1990), 'Vstrecha Kazimera Prunskiene v Moskve', pp. 1, 4; (October 6, 1990), 'Ekonomika: Problemy Baltiiskikh gosudarstv', p. 1.

18. For this quote and the nature of the agreement reached with Gorbachev see *Ekho Litvy* (November 13, 1990), 'Shag k novomu dogovoru', p. 1.

19. A. Sobchak, mayor of Leningrad, who earlier supported republican independence, was fed up with nationalism in December 1990, because nationalism was, among other things, a destabilizing force. See Sedikh, I. (December 12, 1990), 'Cherezvychaina situatsia trebuet cherezvychainykh mer', *Ekho Litvy*, p. 6.

5 Lithuania Plays the Russia Card: Lithuanian-Russian Relations and the USSR

Introduction

The policy of inter-republican cooperation was pursued by the Russian government persistently. It must have seen the process as producing intended results. If the aim of the policy was to make it difficult for Gorbachev to rebuild the Soviet state, then its impact should be visible in the Lithuanian case. In other words, Russia was creating opportunities for Lithuania to hold on to its position. The RSFSR's strategy was complicating the centre's effort to handle the Lithuanian situation. Focusing on Lithuanian-USSR relations, more precisely on Lithuanian-Union negotiations, I scrutinize how Lithuania used Russian support to its advantage.

Lithuania and the USSR were engaged in a lengthy process of negotiations throughout the period June 1990-August 1991. During the negotiation process the Union government was firm on one goal: making Lithuania remain within the Soviet Union. However, its vision of the nature of the ties changed over time. Lithuania, on the other hand, participated in the negotiations with varying goals in mind. The negotiations themselves went through three phases. In each of the phases the influence of Lithuanian-Russian relations on Lithuania's negotiating stance could be clearly observed.

The first phase

The period June 1990-October 1990 constitutes the first phase of the

Lithuanian-USSR negotiations. In June, negotiations had not yet begun. There were efforts on both sides to begin negotiations. October is roughly the time when the Lithuanian leaders were strongly feeling they had been let down by their Russian allies and their orientations to the negotiations changed.

It was clear to the Lithuanian government from early on that Russia was interested in conducting direct relations with Lithuania. Russia's willingness to establish good neighborly relations with Lithuania had significant impact on Lithuania's negotiating posture. It accentuated the division in the Lithuanian leadership. The moderates got a Russian card which would help them reach a settlement with the USSR more in line with Lithuanians' demand to be independent. The radical nationalists found in Russia the partner with whom to negotiate, who could substitute for the centre.

The Union leaders' aim was to use numerous carrots and negotiate and slowly persuade Lithuania to remain associated with the new Union in some form. But Russia's entry as an actor with its policy of supporting republican demands made Lithuania intransigent vis-a-vis the centre. The centre lost its leverage in negotiations with Lithuania. Lithuania became an unyielding negotiating partner. That is the theme I will develop throughout this chapter. By scrutinizing the negotiations process, I will demonstrate how Lithuania's position varied with the pace of development of Lithuanian-Russian relations.

Russia's inclination to come out in favour of Lithuanian independence strengthened the radical nationalists in the Lithuanian leadership, those based in the legislature, V. Landsbergis, B. Kuzmitskas, Ch. Stankevichius, K. Moteika, to name the more prominent members. The moderates, K. Prunskiene, the Prime Minister, and her cabinet -- especially the Foreign Minister A. Saudargas -- found something in Russia's cooperative policy which they could use in their negotiations with the centre.[1] But the nationalists chose Russia as the appropriate negotiations partner instead of the centre and they behaved accordingly in the first phase.

Interpreting the signals

The Union government wanted Lithuania to declare a moratorium on its declaration of sovereignty on March 11, 1990, before any negotiations could begin. Nikolai Ryzhkov, the Soviet Prime Minister, clarified that the centre was being lenient by not demanding a repeal of the declaration as desired by the Congress of the People's Deputies. Prime Minister Prunskiene accepted Moscow's viewpoint. She saw it as inclined to negotiate and understood it as saying that once the moratorium was announced the economic blockade would be lifted. She was ready to propose a moratorium to the Lithuanian legislature, the Supreme Council (Soviet).² She held the opinion that a strong powerful state like the USSR should not be pressured too much. In her words, Lithuania should be flexible and even modest in its demands. Since pressure could be counter-productive, seeking compromise would be useful, she felt.

Foreign Minister A. Saudargas had similar views. He saw progress in Lithuanian-USSR relations. In his opinion, Gorbachev should not be further pressured because that would be harmful for the whole country. Putting Gorbachev in a difficult position by intensifying nationalist demands could bring negative consequences for all of the USSR because of the conservative forces lurking behind him. Lithuania would not be able to escape the effects. He felt optimistic that the moderates in the Lithuanian government would prevail.³

Prunskiene consistently found the centre willing to be forthcoming and reach an agreement with Lithuania. The USSR would like Lithuania to be involved in the new Union but there were different ways to be involved. At times she seemed willing to accept some kind of link with the Union in exchange of a settlement at the state level. Her reason for wanting that was -- Lithuania's position could worsen. The West had already made clear that it would not interfere in case of a conflict between the USSR and Lithuania. Lithuania also needed to negotiate with the centre because unexpected things could happen in Russia. She and a team had worked, she disclosed, from 1989 on different specific issues, e.g., control over the economy, property issues, borders, the army, minorities etc., for negotiations with the centre. The centre also wanted to settle specific issues.

Prunskiene was accused of kowtowing to Moscow but then her successor G. Vagnarius, an opponent of Prunskiene, too was denounced later for becoming pragmatic. It was the need to run the economy and the day to day administration which forced the Prime Minister to be more down to earth.

In marked contrast to the conciliatory position of the Lithuanian cabinet, the legislative leadership took the opposing stance. Russia had started making overtures around this time. Landsbergis was trying to ally Lithuania with Russia as soon as the Russian federation elections were over. It was not one sided but mutual. The newly elected Russian leadership made it known that it viewed Lithuania's wish to be independent favourably. V. Landsbergis, Ch. Stankevichius, B. Kuzmitskas, K. Moteika, and other leaders of the legislature were more interested in negotiating with Russia and signing agreements with Russia rather than the USSR. Academician Vilkas, a member of the parliament, remarked that Lithuania under Landsbergis's leadership was waiting for the USSR to fall apart, and as that happened Lithuania would negotiate with Russia. Russia was being very generous by offering to sell goods at lower than world price.[4]

Landsbergis's reading of what the centre wanted was always negative. He found, again and again, the USSR government inexorable. In his speeches before the Supreme Council he characterized the central government's orientation as hard line and inflexible as before.[5] At the same time Prunskiene found Gorbachev and Ryzhkov to be saying once there was a temporary moratorium the blockade would be lifted and negotiations would begin -- a much more positive reading of signals. Prunskiene and Saudargas both stressed that unnecessary pressures should not be put on the USSR by hard line posturing. They favoured a more flexible position that was open to compromise.

Ch. Stankevichius, deputy chair of the legislature, struck a belligerent position when he said he hoped talks would begin soon but the Lithuanian position remains as defined on the 11th of March or in the Sajudis election platform. It was the 11th March independence declaration on which Moscow sought the moratorium. He also quickly mentioned in the same statement that Lithuania would commemorate the 70th anniversary of the peace treaty between Russia and Lithuania, a treaty through which Russia recognized Lithuania as a sovereign state.[6] His juxtaposition of Russia and Lithuanian-USSR relations is revealing.

Landsbergis was opposed to the moratorium. It was only later that he reluctantly accepted the need for it. In a meeting with Gorbachev he explained why it could not be declared whereas Latvia agreed to freeze its declaration. Prunskiene was ready to accept that the Central leaders' willingness to negotiate with Lithuania signified to a certain extent its recognition of Lithuania as another state because Gorbachev had said he would negotiate only with a foreign country. But Landsbergis and his associates did not subscribe to this view. They did not just demonstrate their own inclinations but also represented the views of the legislature. As legislative debates demonstrate, most legislators shared the views of the leaders of the legislature. Deputy Matkevicius argued that the political situation in the USSR was very unstable and therefore parallel negotiations should be conducted with Soviet republics and especially Russia. Deputy Rasimivicius pointed out that only if the USSR could be made to call Lithuania the Republic of Lithuania rather than the Lithuanian SSR then the problem would be solved. There would be no need to negotiate with the USSR.[7] For deputy Matkevicius, openly calling for negotiations only with Russia was problematic because, as we shall see, there were domestic and foreign pressures to negotiate with the Soviet Union.

Obstruction and delay

What was really significant in the negotiation process, or rather preparations for negotiations, was not so much how the Russia advocates in the Lithuanian leadership were interpreting Gorbachev's or Ryzhkov's intent. What affected the process more seriously were their efforts to impede negotiations with the USSR. They used a number of tactics to do that. One tactic was to try to take the negotiating process out of the control of the Lithuanian government, the cabinet that is. Prunskiene had expected the government would form the Lithuanian delegation for negotiations with the USSR and she made preparations with that in mind. But Landsbergis and other legislators wanted the legislature to conduct the negotiations through delegation of authority. The negotiations were going to be on the parliamentary level, not on intergovernmental level as interstate negotiations normally are.

Prime Minister Prunskiene adamantly opposed the Supreme Council's desire to negotiate. The Council had an ingrained attitude towards the Soviet Union and that would predetermine the nature of the negotiations -- she held. The Council would not be able to take advantage of the lenient disposition of the Ryzhkov cabinet. Besides, the government had worked out the specifics of the topics for negotiations. Landsbergis wanted to head the negotiation team and about that Prunskiene remarked, 'Landsbergis is an MP, he cannot negotiate as a minister can. Negotiations take place between equal partners'.[8] Prunskiene even did not want a mixed delegation of government representatives and legislators. The Justice Minister, though not as sternly as her, held similar views. Minister of Justice, Pranas Kuris, also an expert on international law, maintained that ministries should negotiate. Landsbergis clung to his view that the whole Lithuania was being governed by the Supreme Council, if it negotiated there should not be any problem. Deputy G. Vagnarius, who became Prime Minister of Lithuania after Prunskiene had resigned, identified with Landsbergis's position and said that leaders of the government should not be allowed to control the negotiations.

The Soviet side created a government level negotiations team. Ryzhkov told Prunskiene beforehand that he would be heading the Soviet delegation and asked Lithuania to form an adequate delegation. He clearly preferred a government delegation and said it would be better if Lithuania sent a government level delegation because many specific issues would have to be tackled. The Soviet Prime Minister waited for an answer from the Lithuanian government on the level of negotiations as the infighting prevented the Lithuanians from a prompt response.

The resistance of Prunskiene and her cabinet not withstanding, the government lost out to the legislature which passed a resolution outlining the negotiation procedures to be followed by the Lithuanian side. The Legislature determined that a commission on preparation would set out to prepare for the talks. Landsbergis as the chair of the legislature had the power to name this commission, which he did. Prunskiene was not to head the Commission, B. Kuzmitskas was. B. Kuzmitskas, we have seen, was one of the fervent supporters of the pro-Russia policy. Prunskiene was not even on the Commission.[9]

The Lithuanian Supreme Council gave Landsbergis and Prunskiene the task to create a delegation for negotiations with the Union government. Prunskiene alleged that Landsbergis, in an underhanded manner, was trying to exclude her from the Lithuanian delegation and form the delegation himself without any input from her. A deputy of the Council confirmed that indeed Landsbergis alone submitted the names of the members of the Lithuanian delegation for legislative approval and the list did not include Prunskiene.[10] Prunskiene believed that there were attempts not to include the foreign minister A. Saudargas as well.

The legislative control over the negotiation and shunting aside the government which had all the paperwork ready was one aspect of a strategy to avoid negotiations with Moscow. Some delaying tactics were used as well. First there was the issue of the moratorium. Action was delayed on the moratorium. Ryzhkov was surprised that Lithuanians did not call a special session of the parliament on the moratorium. Influential circles in the United States felt, because of this inaction, Lithuania did not want to reach a compromise with the Soviet Union. Prunskiene wanted a moratorium declared without further delay. E. Bichkauskas, the permanent representative of Lithuania in Moscow and a moderate, also wanted the moratorium quickly approved because further procrastination would be harmful.

The purpose behind the creation of a preparatory Commission was to relegate the issue of negotiations into a procedural thicket. There were to be numerous small groups and other Commissions which would work on specific issues. The preparatory Commission would oversee the works of those bodies. The Lithuanian side then would contact the Soviet side so the Soviets could form such small groups. This amounted to Lithuania wanting to tell the Soviet side what their procedures should be. When Landsbergis was asked if the other side had formed such groups, he replied in the negative and added that things had to proceed little by little. He and his colleagues kept telling the media that negotiations could not begin quickly because time was needed to decide what kind of delegation would represent the two sides, what kind of powers they would have, and where the negotiating table would be set up. 'There is obviously quite some time to go before official talks start', was a typical remark of Landsbergis on the onset of negotiations.[11] The time was needed to prepare comprehensively, he explained. His deputy, Kuzmitskas, observed that it would be good if talks could start but Lithuania had a lot of preparatory work.[12]

One of the tactics was to assert that the USSR delegation had the competence to discuss only economic matters. As one Lithuanian observer noted, the USSR delegation included the head of the KGB, the Chairman of the Belarusian Council of Ministers who could discuss Belarusian-Lithuanian borders, and representatives of the ministry of Defence. They were not there to discuss only economic issues (Siaurusiavichius, August 1, 1990, p. 3).

The supporters of the Russian line made it clear that they preferred to negotiate with Russia and Russia was a better partner. Landsbergis once remarked 'Maybe Russia will be a more realistic partner for negotiations than the USSR' (Siaurusiavichius, August 1, 1990, p. 3). In a press conference, K. Moteika, deputy chairman of the legislature, made the observation that the USSR was coming to negotiate reluctantly not like a state with another state but as the metropolis with its colony. Both he and a colleague, Kuzmitskas, asserted that Russia was very serious about negotiations. To underscore their choice of Russia as the proper negotiating partner under the circumstances they decided to observe the 70th anniversary of the signing of the 1920 peace treaty between Lithuania and Russia.

The Russian side played its part. Unofficial sources floated the rumour that Boris Yeltsin would visit Vilnius. In addition, the signing of the 1920 treaty was solemnly commemorated in a special session of the legislature on July 12, 1990, with an official Russian delegation headed by a member of the presidium of the Supreme Soviet of Russia attending. The prominent figures from the Lithuanian legislature delivered speeches, particularly Landsbergis and Kuzmitskas, speeches that were replete with effusive praise for the Russian government and the Russian people.

Withstanding domestic and foreign pressure

At a time when the Soviet Union wanted to reach a settlement with Lithuania part of the Lithuanian government was able to stall the beginning of talks. It was possible for Landsbergis and like-minded legislative leaders to successfully use delaying moves because they had decided to cast their fate with Russia. They could do that because Russia had adopted its policy to supplant the centre in centre-republican relations. It is true that the more nationalistic elements in the Lithuanian leadership would probably have resisted negotiations with the centre. But the pressure that was brought to bear upon them was too intense for them to withstand if there had not been Russian support.

This pressure did not simply come from the Union government in the form of the blockade and urging to remain a part of the Soviet federation. It also came from pragmatic Lithuanian government leaders such as the Prime Minister and her cabinet, the Lithuanian press, Lithuanian intellectuals, and western countries.[13]

The Lithuanian media were dismayed at the turn of events. They attacked Landsbergis for leading the leadership astray on such an important foreign policy matter as talks with the Soviet Union. A number of political observers castigated the legislators for themselves using delaying tactics while accusing the centre of doing that or for relying too much on Yeltsin and Russia though it was hard to imagine Yeltsin quarrelling with Gorbachev for Lithuania (Kirkilas, September 19, 1990, p. 3; Kashis, September 5, 1990, p. 3). Lithuanian intellectuals appealed to the government to negotiate with the USSR. Twenty prominent Lithuanian intellectuals signed an appeal to the people of Lithuania. A group of Supreme Council deputies also signed. Many of the signers were active members of the Sajudis. This appeal stated that the Supreme Council was continually expanding its power and taking over the authority of the Council of Ministers. About the negotiations with the USSR the appeal stated, 'Certain sectors of society and even Supreme Soviet deputies are seeking pretexts to delay the start of talks or even not to start them altogether'.[14] In addition to pressure from the intelligentsia there were concerns expressed by the informed public. The Lithuanian newspaper, *Ekho Litvy*, received numerous letters from its readers who were worried about their government's dilatory tactics regarding talks with the Soviet Union.

Western countries, primarily the United States and Great Britain, did not want Lithuania to destabilize the USSR at that particular stage of the reform process. Their chief concern was Lithuania might jeopardize Gorbachev's position when he was trying to take the country in a market and democratic direction in the face of conservative resistance.[15] When Lithuanian leaders approached western leaders they were told that stability in the Soviet Union was important and difficulties should not be created for Gorbachev. Lithuania had expected financial backing from the west but it did not materialize (Shved, November 22, 1990, p. 2). The Western countries were also denying Lithuanian requests to be formally included into any Western groupings. The second CSCE Human Dimension Conference rejected Lithuania's plea to be granted observer status at the conference. The more radical nationalists felt that they had to at least create the semblance of negotiations with the USSR because the West practically demanded it.

While Landsbergis and his colleagues employed delaying tactics regarding official talks with the USSR, they tried to swiftly improve relations with the RSFSR. Lithuania proceeded fast to build ties with Russia at a time when even preliminary consultations had not yet begun with the USSR government, much less formal negotiations. Landsbergis urged the legislature to act quickly on negotiations with Russia which it did. He told the legislature that if there had been a treaty between Lithuania and Russia, the economic blockade would not have been working.

The second phase

The second phase of talks between Lithuania and the Soviet Union covers the end of 1990, roughly the period from October 1990 till early January 1991. This period was characterized by Lithuania finally becoming prepared for negotiations with the centre, a considerable shift in Lithuania's negotiating stance, a slight hardening of the central government's position, and a Lithuanian sense of being in an uncertain position as regards its relations with Russia.

Members of the Lithuanian Council of Ministers including the Prime Minister kept up the pressure on the Lithuanian legislature to negotiate with the USSR. The Vice Premier R. Ozolas at one point remarked that the USSR had done more for Lithuania's secession than Lithuania herself had.[16] But these efforts were fruitless. Landsbergis went ahead and proposed a Lithuanian delegation to the parliament which did not even include the prime minister. It was only when the Lithuanian leaders, particularly the legislative ones, began sensing uncertainty in the political atmosphere that they began to relent.

The Lithuanian government leaders, being careful monitors of relations between Russia and the Union authorities noticed relatively early the beginning of a rapprochement between the centre and the RSFSR. Prunskiene was the first high level official to note that. This beginning of the rapprochement took on special significance for Lithuania and was reflected in its attitudes toward the central government. The Lithuanian government first noted that there were improvements in relations between the centre and Russia. It felt a new political environment was taking shape. The emerging relations were not at all clear cut yet. The centre and the Russian leaders had formed a joint committee to hasten transition to a market economy. What the competence of the centre and Russia would be was not clear yet.

This feeling of uncertainty started to force some changes into its Russia centred policy of external relations. It was declared that since politics was so fluid Lithuania would maintain relations with those who could deliver goods to it. But preference would be given to those who would recognize

Lithuania as a sovereign state. Now Lithuania was acknowledging the need to negotiate with anybody who could claim control over resources. This was Prunskiene's position all along. Aside from this formal declaration of policy by the government there was another important event. Finally the delegation for negotiations with the USSR was approved and the delegation contained not only Prunskiene herself but also the foreign minister whom Prunskiene wanted to be on the delegation.[17]

The second phase coincided with the period when Lithuania felt isolated from Russia and intensely lobbied western governments for support. There were hardly any interactions with the Russian government or the Russian democrats. It was a difficult time for Lithuania. Its leaders were fearing armed attacks by the Soviet Union. Their fear was demonstrated by the joint session of the three Baltic legislatures held in Vilnius to which no representatives of the Russian government went although some republics sent theirs. Landsbergis again and again drew attention to creeping hard line control over the central government. He even believed a puppet government to supplant the current Lithuanian authority had already been formed in Moscow. Prunskiene described the situation as a financial war waged both by the centre and Russia against her country. In December Soviet foreign minister, E. Shevardnadze, resigned. His resignation was viewed as the departure of the friend Lithuania had in the USSR government who had opposed use of force against it. It was a time of uncertainty, apprehension, and isolation from an ally on whom many Lithuanian leaders depended much.

Lithuania becomes flexible

In the second phase, Lithuania's more accommodative negotiating approach was manifested through the Council of Ministers' regaining control over the process. Both Prunskiene and her deputy premier Ozolas assumed responsibility.[18] Her contacts with the USSR government and declarations on what Lithuania's position was amounted to reassertion of lost authority. She and vice premier Ozolas wrote the two telegrams the tones of which could not be more subdued. Ozolas wrote to V. Doguzhiev, a member of the USSR delegation and head of the working group created to conduct preparatory sessions before negotiations, 'After you broke the meeting of the working group following the Supreme Soviet debate, I have not received any new information. I hope for quick information. We are ready to work.'[19] Prunskiene wrote to Ryzhkov and Iu. Masliukov, the chair of the Gosplan, '...We express readiness to participate immediately in the consideration and resolution of these problems at a time convenient to you.'[20]

The shifts in the position of the legislative leaders were more striking in view of the fact that they had stridently denounced the Union government for holding on to an imperial orientation and considering Lithuania still a part of the USSR. It was Landsbergis who had epitomized the orientation of the more nationalist position of the legislative leaders who displayed the changes. At the end of September 1990, he said it seemed to him the USSR would not try to persuade Lithuania to sign this or that treaty (meaning the Union Treaty). Whereas in the first phase he felt that was what the USSR wanted to do. After the first consultative session between the two negotiating teams, he thought the hindrances resulted not from any malevolence on the part of the centre but because of simple stereotyping! It just could not still get rid of the tendency to view Lithuania as one of the republics.[21] There was also an effort to present a unified softened position on negotiations. Landsbergis and Prunskiene signed a declaration in which they denounced the fanning of ethnic hatred in Lithuania by some in association with conservative forces in the USSR in an attempt to sabotage the negotiations between Lithuania and the USSR which had just begun.

What signified most clearly Lithuania's desire now to negotiate seriously with the centre was a resolution passed by the Supreme Council. This resolution allowed the negotiating team to operate without a protocol of negotiations.[22] This was the protocol on which, the Lithuanians had demanded earlier, must be agreement before negotiations could begin. The protocol drafted by Lithuania was thought to be an obstacle to negotiations by the USSR. The resolution was a major concession on Lithuania's part. It now wanted to negotiate like a responsible partner and accepted the Union government as a partner. Indeed a number of meetings were held between the working groups that were formed to conduct preliminary talks before the state delegations themselves met. A meeting between the state delegations was held and more meetings were going to be held. Such an atmosphere persisted when the Soviet army took over the radio and television tower in Lithuania and there were black beret attacks in Latvia in January, 1991. After the attacks circumstances changed radically and the third phase began in the Lithuanian-USSR negotiations.

The third phase

When January 1991 began, Lithuania was feeling thoroughly isolated; so much so that Landsbergis said it should capitulate to Moscow because it had failed to enlist serious western support and was now in total isolation. He added there was increasing discord among Lithuanian parliamentarians and

74 Inter-republican cooperation

some wanted to remove him.[23] The year 1990 saw a general albeit gradual turn by Gorbachev to the right. He acquired more and more power for an already strong presidency and his rhetoric came to emphasize law and order, discipline etc. (Sharlet, 1992, pp. 85-118). In December 1990, some observers found Gorbachev to be swinging too far to the right and too fast.[24] Some predicted he would soon use the KGB and the military to enforce order.

The attacks and Russian reactions

It was around this time that the RSFSR reached agreement with the centre on the budget and the issue of stabilizing the social and economic situation in the country. It agreed to contribute 80 billion rubles to the Union budget, considerably more than the 23 billion proposed by the Russian parliament but much less than the 143 billion given the year before. Yeltsin said after signing the agreement, 'We had to sign the agreement. If Russia had not signed, that would of course be a very serious step toward the collapse of the Union -- one which we cannot permit'.[25] At the same time, several divisions of soldiers were going to be moved to the Baltic area at Defence Minister D. Yazov's order to enforce Soviet military conscription. Yeltsin's response was almost muted. He did not oppose such enforcement in the Baltic specifically but voiced opposition to forcible conscription in general.

But the armed attacks on Lithuania in January 11-13, 1991, became a turning point in both Lithuanian-Russian relations and centre-Russian relations. Shortly after the attacks Yeltsin called for the resignation of Gorbachev because he had brought the USSR to the brink of dictatorship. In a gesture of support and solidarity Yeltsin went to Estonia and attended its legislative session. He thought the attacks on the Baltic republics were a powerful assault against democracy. The right was pushing the Central government toward use of force and abandoning democratic means.[26] R. Khasbulatov, the Deputy Chairman of the Russian parliament said that the conservative cabinet forced Gorbachev to adopt the policy he had adopted. Gorbachev had better gain some perspective, else events would develop in such a way that it would sweep away not only the democratic forces but also Gorbachev himself.[27] RSFSR minister of the Press and Mass Media, M. Poltoranin described the Lithuanian events as an attempted coup. He drew a parallel between these and the military intervention in 1968 calling upon the west to support the Baltic republics and Russia and not to supply Gorbachev with aid.[28]

It was not only the Russian government from which strong condemnation ensued. It came from the Russian democratic forces as well.

A plenum of the Council of Representatives of Democratic Russia decided to engage in a political strike and other protest activities. The slogans of the strike would be, 'The resignation of the USSR president and his team', 'Withdrawal of troops from Lithuania' etc. Members of Democratic Russia held demonstrations demanding the situation in Lithuania be normalized.[29] Leningrad's reformist Mayor, A. Sobchak, called for a special session of the USSR Congress of People's Deputies to which the President should be called upon to report on the Baltic events. Lithuania and Russia were back in a close alliance. This time the relations were even closer than before the lapse in late 1990. This was going to have an influence on the ruptured negotiation process.

Lithuania turns to Russia again

The result of the January attacks was Lithuania's explicit, unconcealed, and in terms of different elements in the leadership near complete turn to the RSFSR. A. Saudargas who was still Foreign Minister even though Prunskiene had resigned, asserted that Gorbachev was no longer in power and the army and the secret service was reestablishing their power in the USSR. Saudargas was a pragmatic advocate of negotiations with the USSR but he too became a supporter of the Russia policy of the nationalists. He now thought that Yeltsin genuinely wanted to change the system.[30] The leadership of the Baltic republics in general came to hold the view that Gorbachev was no longer exercising authority in the Central government. Soon after the assault, Landsbergis informed that a treaty with Russia would be signed in just a few days, a treaty that was actually signed at the end of July 1991.

After the Baltic events the USSR government, especially Gorbachev and Foreign Minister A. Bessmertnyk, did their best to dissociate the Soviet leadership from the attacks. Gorbachev told the Soviet parliament that he learned about the events on January the 13th. Bessmertnyk called the Vilnius events tragic. He said they were not a reflection of the USSR's policy and was not welcomed by the leadership.[31]

The Soviet government wanted the talks with Lithuania to resume. Gorbachev displayed interest in when Lithuania would start negotiations again. But even though he wanted to distance himself from the application of military force and was eager to see negotiations begin he displayed a certain sternness when he emphasized that Lithuania needed to leave the Union lawfully. There was pressure on Lithuania to negotiate from the West. At one point the US envoy M. Kempelman was sent to express concern that negotiations had not yet begun.[32]

When Lithuania came to Moscow to talk about the renewal of negotiations it had a much more hardened position than in the immediate past. This stronger negotiating stance was manifested in four ways. First, Lithuania wanted that the security of the Lithuanian government be guaranteed and a declaration against the use of force issued. The Soviet side considered it a prior condition and made it known that it would not negotiate under prior conditions.[33] Second, the Lithuanian side wanted the issue of recognition and inter-state relations settled first which the USSR did not want and it continued to refer to the talks as discussions with a republic. The leader of the USSR negotiating team even said that the aim of the talks was to convince Lithuania to stay in the Union. Third, Lithuania kept blaming the central leaders for the small scale OMON attacks taking place in the months preceding the August coup although the central government said it had disavowed the use of force and tried to distance itself from the force being used. Fourth, again and again Lithuania declared the Soviet Union was not serious about negotiations. Landsbergis told the Lithuanian parliament that he did not believe the centre was interested in genuine negotiations because the Soviet delegation did not have authority to negotiate. Such a charge was used as a delaying tactic in the first phase. But more important than the above was Lithuania's demand that the Union government compensate Lithuania for the damages which had resulted from its occupation by the Soviet Union since 1940.[34]

A few sessions of negotiations were held but they did not amount to anything. Landsbergis said Lithuania was negotiating because the West wanted it to. Actually both Lithuania and the USSR were buying time. It was clear there would be a Union Treaty; Lithuania waited for the new union structures to emerge; so did the USSR.

The centre and its goal

We have seen the centre wanted Lithuania to negotiate and Russia strengthened Lithuania against it. But what were the goals the centre wanted to attain from the negotiations which it could not achieve because Russia created more room for Lithuania to manoeuvre thus enabling it to hold on to a more intransigent position? What was the Soviet Union's negotiation policy which could not be implemented?

After Lithuania revived its independence, the Soviet government took a very legalistic, constitutional position. It was characteristic of Gorbachev's government to resort to legalism on such occasions. It stuck to the position that Lithuania needed to leave the Union according to the provisions of the law on secession. The statements of the Soviet leaders, the types of issues they wanted to negotiate, and the agreements that were reached between Lithuania and the USSR both inside and outside the main negotiation framework are indicative of a number of things.

The Soviet Union did not want Lithuania to leave. But it also did not want it to occupy the old status of a republic in a centralized state. It wanted to keep Lithuania engaged in the negotiation process and make small concessions to it. These concessions implicitly awarded Lithuania the trappings of an independent state. The central government reached agreement on the conscription issue in 1990 which allowed the Lithuanian youth not to join the Soviet army.[35] The USSR Goskompechat permitted Lithuania to print its own postage stamps and use them on the Soviet territory.[36] They signed a few more agreements including some on sports.

The Gorbachev leadership tried to keep Lithuania engaged in negotiations and putatively within the Union till an agreement on the future federation emerged and the political transition began within the constitutional framework. The new Union would be attractive enough to convince the Lithuanians to retain some sort of linkage with it. Even if the Lithuanians did not do that, it would not matter anymore. They were trying to get time, something that Gorbachev acknowledged he did very often (Gorbachev, 1991).

In 1991, it became increasingly clear that the central government was more and more accepting Lithuania as an independent state and buying time. The USSR Minister of Transportation, for instance, visited Lithuania in July 1991, and handed a draft treaty to the Lithuanian government on cooperation in this sector because no general treaty existed yet.[37] There were negotiations going on between Lithuania and the Commission for Aeronavigation of the USSR Council of Ministers about use of USSR air space for civilian flights and Lithuania seemed optimistic about getting permission.

Conclusion

This chapter has traced the impact of Russia's cooperation on Lithuania-USSR relations by focusing on the negotiations between Lithuania and the Soviet Union. My goal was to show how Russia was actually lowering the centre's control over centre-periphery relations. By analysing the different phases of the negotiation process I have demonstrated how Lithuania's orientation coincided with its understanding of the nature of Russian support.

In both the first and third phases of negotiations Lithuania felt Russia was going to come out in its support very strongly. Consequently, Lithuania adopted an unaccommodative posture toward the Union, an inflexible position. There were intra-government conflicts in the first phase but in the third phase they nearly disappeared. In the third phase the armed attacks on the radio and television tower caused renewed and stronger support from Russia and the explicit hardening of Lithuania's position.

The second phase shows Lithuania more yielding with the advocates of negotiations ascending inside the government. This was the time when the Lithuanian leaders felt very much isolated, and feared military attacks from the centre. It was also the period when Russia was negotiating with the centre on the formation of a coalition government and reaching agreements on important subjects. No statement of support was issued by Russia for a Lithuania that was living in fear and isolation.

As for the central leaders, they wanted to put together the blueprint for a new Union with Lithuania still in it. In addition, they wanted to appear to be capable enough to manage their relations with this republic. Both of these goals could not be achieved even though there was western support largely because of Russia's inter-republican politics.

Notes

1. See *Vilnius International Service* (May 31, 1990), 'Prunskiene on Prospects for Negotiations'; translated in *FBIS* (June 1, 1990), p. 63.

2. *Ekho Litvy* (June 27, 1990), 'Press Konferentsia', p. 1.

3. *ADN International Service* (June 6, 1990), 'Foreign Minister Seeks Treaty with USSR'; translated in the *FBIS* (June 6, 1990), p. 74.

4. *Ekho Litvy* (August 1, 1990), ' Aktual'noe interv'iu: Luchshaya politika -- pravda', pp. 1, 2.

5. See for instance, *Ekho Litvy* (June 30, 1990), 'Vystuplenie Vitautasa Landsbergisa', pp. 1, 2.

6. *Vilnius Domestic Service* (July 4, 1990), 'Official Views Talks'; translated in *FBIS*, July 5, 1990, p. 73.

7. *Vilnius Domestic Service* (July 10, 1990), '10 July Lithuanian Supreme Council Session Reported'; translated in *FBIS* (July 11, 1990), p. 40.

8. For this remark and her general opposition see, *FBIS* (July 5, 1990), 'Prunskiene Views Preparations', p. 74; *Vilnius Domestic Service* (July 5, 1990), 'Reportage on Negotiations over Talks with Moscow'; translated in *FBIS* (July 5, 1990), p. 72.

9. *Vilnius Domestic Service* (July 12, 1990), 'Landsbergis on Negotiations'; translated in *FBIS* (July 12, 1990), p. 53.

10. *Ekho Litvy* (August 16, 1990), 'Parliamentariam nado otdykha', pp. 1, 2.

11. *TASS* (July 11, 1990), 'Landsbergis Says Official Talks Still Far Away'; published in the *FBIS* (July 12, 1990), p. 55.

12. *Ekho Litvy* (July 26, 1990), 'Press Konferentsia', p. 1.

13. The Central government did not simply use economic pressure, it appealed to the people of Lithuania as well. For the appeal of the Presidium of the Supreme Soviet of the USSR see, *Ekho Litvy* (July 21, 1990), ' Prizyv k dialogu', p. 1.

14. *Izvestia* (August 4, 1990), 'Appeal Could Wreck Independence Process'; translated in *FBIS* (August 7, 1990), p. 56. On who were the people making the appeal see, *Moscow Television Service* (August 6, 1990), 'Lithuanian Intelligentsia Criticizes Council'; translated in *FBIS* (August 7, 1990), p. 56.

15. On the theme of western countries not wanting to jeopardize Gorbachev's reform and create instability in the USSR by supporting Lithuania in deed see the following reports in *Ekho Litvy* (July 17, 1990), 'Deiatel'nost pravitel'stva Litvy: Cherti pervogo etapa', pp. 1, 2; (September 25, 1990), 'Vstrecha v Kremle', p. 1; (November 30, 1990), 'Doklad Kazimeri Prunskiene v Tsurike', pp. 1, 2.

16. *TASS* (August 13, 1990), 'Lithuania's Ozolas Views Talks with USSR'; published in *FBIS* (August 14, 1990), p. 52. For deputy premier A. Brazauskas urging the parliament to negotiate see reports on his speech to the parliament, *Vilnius Domestic Service* (August 21, 1990), 'Brazauskas Speaks on Talks'; translated in *FBIS*, August 21, 1990, p. 64.

17. *Ekho Litvy* (August 23, 1990), 'Postanovlenie Verkhovnogo Sovieta Litovskoi Respubliki ob utvorzhdenii chlenov gosudarstvennoi delegatsii Litovskoi Respubliki', p. 1.

18. See the following two reports in the *Ekho Litvy* (September 28, 1990), 'Litva-USSR: Vstrecha 2 Oktiabria', p. 1; (October 2, 1990), 'Uspekhov na peregovorakh', p. 1.

19. For the text of the telegram see *Ekho Litvy* (November 21, 1990), 'Telegrama R. Ozolasa V. Doguzhievu', p. 1.

20. *Ekho Litvy* (November 23, 1990), 'Telegrama K. Prunskiene N. Ryzhkovu i Iu. Masliukovu', p. 1.

21. *Ekho Litvy* (October 6, 1990), 'Ob itogakh konsul'tativnogo soveshchania i peregovorakh s Sovietskim Soyuzom', p. 1.

22. *Ekho Litvy* (December 29, 1990), 'Postanovlenie Verkhovnogo Soveta Litovskoi Respubliki o mezhgosudarstvennom peregovorakh mezhdu Litovskoi Respublikoi i Soiuzom SSR', p. 1.

23. *TASS* (January 4, 1991), 'Landsbergis: Lithuania Should "Capitulate"'; translated in *FBIS* (January 7, 1991), p. 43.

24. *Jerusalem Domestic Service* (December 30, 1990), 'Afanasyev: Gorbachev on Verge of Dictatorship'; translated in *FBIS* (January 2, 1991), p. 27.

25. *Moscow Domestic Service* (January 9, 1991), 'Yeltsin Reviews Gorbachev Talks'; translated in *FBIS* (January 10, 1991), p. 66.

26. For his visit to Estonia see *FBIS* (January 14, 1991), 'Yeltsin Attends Session', p. 99; for his remarks see *TASS* (January 19, 1991), 'Says Right Pressuring Gorbachev', published in *FBIS* (January 15, 1991), p. 89.

27. *ADN* (January 14, 1991), 'Official Says Gorbachev Forced into Policies'; translated in *FBIS* (January 15, 1991), p. 91.

28. *DPA* (January 20, 1991), 'Minister Urges West to Halt Aid to Gorbachev'; translated in *FBIS* (January 23, 1991), p. 97.

29. For reactions from Democratic Russia see *TASS* (January 13, 1991), 'Democratic Russia Calls for Gorbachev Resignation', translated in *FBIS* (January 14, 1991), p. 25; *Moscow World Service* (January 15, 1991), 'Democratic Russia Views Reactionary Onslaught', translated in *FBIS* (January 15, 1991), p. 42.

30. *Der Morgen* (January 16, 1991) 'Saudargas: Military Junta Ordered Action', p. 3; translated in *FBIS* (January 18, 1991), p. 56. Also see *ADN* (January 15, 1991), 'Asserts Gorbachev Not in Control'; translated in *FBIS* (January 16, 1991), p. 65.

31. *TASS* (January 14, 1991), 'Gorbachev Learned of Vilnius Events 13th January'; published in *FBIS* (January 15, 1991), p. 24. Also see *Moscow Domestic Service* (January 16, 1991), 'Bessmertnyk: Vilnius Events Do Not Reflect Policy'; translated in *FBIS* (January 16, 1991), p. 61.

32. *Ekho Litvy* (March 29, 1991), 'O vozmozhnostiakh peregovorov', p. 1.

33. Sheinberg, M. (March 30, 1991), 'Shto s peregovorami?', *Ekho Litvy*, p. 1. A member of the Central Committee of the CPSU said Lithuania's laying down conditions did not help, they were ultimatums, see *Ekho Litvy* (April 10, 1991), 'Mezhdu slukhami i real'nosti', p. 3, under Daidzhest Pressa Litvy. The Soviet response should also be understood keeping in mind its attempts to distance itself from the attacks themselves.

34. See Landsbergis's speech in *Ekho Litvy* (June 6, 1991), 'Na sessii Verkhovnogo Soveta Respubliki', p. 1.

35. But Lithuania could not prevent them from joining if they wanted to join.

36. *Ekho Litvy* (February 7, 1991), 'Litovskie pochtovye marki vypushchenye na voliu', p. 3. Although the exact date for the issuance of the permit is not given, it seems very likely it was given in 1990.

37. *Ekho Litvy* (July 27, 1991), 'V interesakh sotrudnichestva', p. 1. Gorbachev was trying to extricate himself from the embrace of the hard liners in early 1991.

6 Through the Eyes of the Russian Government: Content Analysis of Elite Pronouncements

Introduction

During the September 1994 Russian-US summit Russian President Boris Yeltsin sternly asserted that the CIS states, '... are our neighbours. Yesterday we lived in the same house, in the Soviet Union. They are our blood, right? Come on, let's be honest'. Western observers have noted with a degree of disbelief that Russia has been rather inflexible about its role of influence in the former Soviet republics. John Dunlop (1993) thought it odd that Yeltsin was supporting Gorbachev and playing the role of the 'Velvet' emperor after the August 1991 coup failed. But if we take a close look at what Yeltsin and some important members of the Russian government thought about Russia's relations with the Soviet republics during the period covered by this study, June 1990-August 1991, we would not have reason to be puzzled by Russian behaviour in late 1991 or the present.

One of the aspects of the cooperative process studied here was what the participants themselves said what they thought it was. The Russian elites kept making statements about their cooperation as a whole or its components as the process itself was developing. These statements were descriptive, explanatory, and evaluative. They were general and specific. I will study these elite utterances using content analysis as the method with a view to understand the RSFSR's inter-republican cooperation policy from the elite's vantage point.

Content analysis of Soviet era politicians is not new. Several successful studies have been done using pre-Gorbachev media material. This study will be based on the reports of a much freer media. Soviet period politicians were especially careful about their public pronouncements. The Russian elite, which was really an offshoot of the traditional Soviet elite, was very similar. These were not amateur politicians; they were very familiar with a life where a decision makers' pronouncements and gestures were carefully observed and interpreted. They were fully aware of the symbolic value of words and themes and the practical necessity of choosing them with care.

The first part of the chapter details the method used in the study, the second part presents the data and analyses them, the conclusion summarizes the results and relates them to the results of the previous four chapters.

Method

Different types of content analyses are done depending upon the research questions. Starting from word count they could range to enumeration of relatively complex themes expressed in a cluster of sentences spanning more than one paragraph. Content analyses of mass media coverage of topics have focused on pictures and their contents. My goal is to select the themes the Russian leaders used to represent their cooperative manoeuvres. I seek to find out what they thought this cooperation was, should be, was leading to, and then study the pattern those views form. This will supplement the analyses done in other chapters. Using content analysis to supplement other modes of analysis is common (Krippendorf, 1980).

Validity

The question of validity is always a nagging one in content analysis. As Weber has pointed out, because content analysis relies heavily on face validity many social scientists view the results with skepticism (Weber, 1985, p. 19). Validity of course deals with the issue of whether the method being used is appropriate and the measures being used are correctly measuring the variables representing the concepts. According to Weber (1985, p. 18), 'To assert that a research result based on content analysis is valid is to assert that the finding does not depend upon, or is generalizable beyond the specific data, methods, or measurements of a particular study'. In arguing that content analysis is a valid method to tap Russian leaders' attitudes towards Russia's inter-republican cooperation, I will present some information as well as suggest some validity tests.

The news media on which the analysis is based were the media of 1990 and 1991 not those of the pre-reform era. Gorbachev's policy of Glasnost had a number of years to bring about changes in the manner the media covered political events and politicians. The Russian government was trying to establish itself as an alternative to the more restrictive, secretive, and wily central government. It was presenting itself as more open, truthful, and responsible. Lying constantly about a major policy initiative was not going to help it project itself as a more credible source of information.

The RSFSR's inter-republican cooperation strategy dealt with an issue of utmost importance, the nature of the Soviet state. The politicians making public statements about such an issue would be circumspect. They could do a number of things by being careless, one of which would be raising the expectations of the republics to an unacceptably high level. The statements being, in most cases, about legal documents -- such as agreements or treaties -- officials could not risk making false statements since such utterances are used later in interpreting legal documents. The leaders whose statements were selected were not just any high level Russian government officials but those who were directly involved in making and implementing the cooperation policy.

A number of validity tests can be applied to the analysis. One way of finding out whether the analysis has validity is to compare its results to the findings contained in other chapters in the book. If the findings converge or are similar then the method used here could be considered valid. I will compare the findings with those in other chapters in the conclusion. The test of hypothesis validity could also be applied. According to this validity test if the findings of a content analysis correspond to the hypothesis and the theoretical orientation of the study, the research approach is valid. I will see how the results of this study correspond to the theoretical orientation and the articulated theses.[1]

The units of analysis

The sampling units are the units which contain the data or the recording units.[2] I have not used probability sampling to select the units (sampling units), but aimed for a comprehensive set of the units (sampling units) which would be almost the universe and properly represent the universe. This is not at all unusual.[3] Many analysts have used a comprehensive set rather than sample the whole population.

My units of analysis (sampling units) are the speeches and statements either made exclusively about Russian inter-republican cooperation or parts of which were devoted to this policy. These speeches and statements were made during the period June 1990-August 1991, the period covered by this book. In total, sixty two units were selected. The speeches and statements of the following Russian leaders were perused to select the units of analysis (sampling units):

1. Boris Yeltsin
2. Ivan Silaev
3. Gennady Fil'shin
4. Andrei Kozyrev
5. Ruslan Khasbulatov
6. Alexander Granberg
7. Feodor Shelov-Kovedyaev
8. Valentin Rodionov
9. U.A. Novichkov

The statements of these officials were selected because they were involved in the making and carrying out of the policy. They were the persons who knew most about why Russia was doing what it was doing. Boris Yeltsin was the most important leader in terms of the political reality. Formally he was first the chair of the Russian Supreme Soviet and from June 1991 the President of the Russian Republic. He signed all the most important treaties and many important protocols and declarations. As the highest level government official, he visited Estonia, Kazakhstan, Kyrgyzstan, Latvia, and Ukraine. During those visits he delivered a number of important speeches in which he explained how Russia was relating to the union republics. Aside from these speeches, he talked about this process in speeches to the Russian legislature, pre-election media interviews, and news conferences.

Ivan Silaev was the Russian Prime Minister during the period under consideration. He was the leader who signed the economic agreements that Russia concluded with almost all the republics. Some visits were made by him as well. He made numerous statements at the signing ceremonies even when the signer was not him but Yeltsin as was the case during the signing of the Treaty on the Bases of Inter-State Relations between Belarus and Russia. Silaev gave numerous interviews to the media some of which dealt with inter-republican cooperation. He touched upon the issue in his reports to the Russian legislature.

Gennady Fil'shin is a special case. He was a Russian deputy prime minister. In selecting him, I relied on my knowledge of the policy making environment prevailing in Russia. He was a very high level politician with expertise in economics and talked on a number of occasions about this policy.

I feel he was involved in the articulation of the policy in some way.

Andrei Kozyrev was confirmed as the Russian foreign minister at the end of 1990 and was deeply involved in the process. He attended signing ceremonies and accompanied Yeltsin during his visit to Kyrgyzstan. The Russian Ministry of Foreign Affairs (MID) dealt with the issue in two declarations. Kozyrev wrote an article on this policy.

Ruslan Khasbulatov, the deputy chair of the Russian parliament, was also involved in making and implementing the policy. He went to some republics as part of the Russian delegations. Like Khasbulatov, Alexander Granberg and Feodor Shelov-Kovedyaev were both legislative figures. Granberg headed the Supreme Soviet Committee on Inter-republican Relations and Regional Politics and Shelov-Kovedyaev was the chair of the Supreme Soviet Sub-committee on Inter-republican Cooperation. Radionov and Novichkov, deputy ministers respectively of culture and education, both negotiated and signed agreements in their areas.

Audience bias is a serious concern in any content analysis. This is so because it is assumed that contents of speeches vary according to the audiences they are addressed to. This bias can be reduced by including speeches delivered to different types of audiences rather than just one. The attempt to select a comprehensive set of statements has worked to control for audience bias. These statements were addressed to different kinds of audiences: the publics of a number of republics, i.e., Kazakhstan, Kyrgyzstan, Latvia, Moldova, and Ukraine, the members of the Russian Supreme Soviet, soldiers and instructors at the Dzherzinsky Military Academy, the Russian masses. I have noticed hardly any variation in themes according to the targeted audiences. As a matter of fact, the speech that Yeltsin delivered to the Ukrainian parliament was very similar to the one he gave to the Russian parliament; they matched almost word for word. Two instances of theme selection by audiences that I have noticed were the ones that appeared in Yeltsin's speeches to the Dzherzinsky Academy and to the European parliament. The speech to the Academy emphasized only the continuity themes that is linkage preservation themes. But even then, the way those themes were situated in the text did not distort Russian position expressed in other settings. The European parliament speech contained only economic themes and pro-republic themes but those were not ideas which had not been expressed to other audiences.

The statements and speeches were selected from the following sources: *Ekho Litvy, FBIS, Kazakhstanskaya pravda, Pravda Ukrainy, Pravda vostoka, Rossiiskaya gazeta, Slovo Kyrgyzstana, Sovetskaya Belorussiya, Sovetskaya Moldova*. The large number of newspapers searched control for editorial biases and help make the set of statements more inclusive. An example will demonstrate how important have been the newspapers from the non-Russian republics, Yeltsin's speech given at the signing of the Lithuanian-Russian Treaty on the Bases of Inter-State Relations was not published in the *Rossiiskaya gazeta* but was in *Ekho Litvy*. *Rossiiskaya gazeta* gave the gist of the speech in indirect speech of narration.

The recording units

The recording units of analysis were the themes which were raised in these statements. Theme analysis is considered to be the most complex and intractable kind of content analysis but nonetheless they have been done in political science as well as folklore and other fields.[4] I have followed the Simulation of Interview procedures.[5] My analysis is a little different from the Simulation of Interview situation because these are statements whereas in Simulation of Interviews the text used are written documents of authors. To find out why the Russian leaders were engaging in those cooperative actions I articulated the following questions:

1. Why is Russia performing a particular action or set of actions?
2. What would have happened if Russia was not conducting the action(s)?
3. What is(are) the action(s)?
4. What the action(s) is(are) not?
5. What will this lead to?

Each of the questions were capable of picking up themes specific to the circumstances as well as themes that were general and were applicable to the whole process. They were articulated with the nature of the inquiry in mind and after examining the texts of a number of statements themselves. The first question aimed at themes that the speaker presented as the causes of the Russian government's actions. The second question taps the thinking on the preventive nature of the actions. What was it Russia wanted to prevent by its actions? What would inaction in this policy area portend? This question is the other side of the first question. The third question dealt with the characterization of the process by the Russian elites themselves. Characterization themes are capable of capturing the whole process because they can achieve a high level of generality. The fourth question was the negative version of the third question. The fifth question dealt with the future which the Russian participants expected this process as a whole or a particular action to bring about.

The themes that were selected responded to these questions. Themes are usually expressed in three ways: in a cluster of sentences, in one full sentence, as parts of a compound sentence the elements of which are joined with conjunctions and punctuation marks. It was not unusual to find more than one theme expressed in a sentence.

I collected one theme per statement even though the theme might have occurred more than once in the same unit. One example is Yeltsin's speech to the Russian parliament shortly after the signing of the Treaty on the Bases of Inter-State Relations with Ukraine in November 1990. He said the treaty would lead to Russian investment in Ukrainian industries producing for export to Russia and vise versa, joint investment with foreign companies. Although more than one sentence were used to express the thoughts they constituted the same idea, future close economic relations. The themes occurring in each statement were recorded separately in index cards numbering them in accordance with the order in which they appeared in the statement. If a speech contained four themes the theme which appeared first in the speech was recorded as theme number one and the one appearing last was recorded as theme number four. This was done to detect any deliberate ordering of themes by the speakers. Each card, along with the theme, contained four dimensions on the themes: the name of the speaker, the republic where it was being said, the audience to whom it was being said, and the date.

There were fifty themes expressed with various frequencies. Some examples of the themes which appeared more frequently: this cooperation will lead to a Union, it will lead to an economic union, this is a new page in our relations, we are signing treaties because we want to stabilize the economy or the crisis situation, this is happening because the republics have declared sovereignty, Russia is joining the defence line of the republics through this. Since there was a large number of themes I devised a categorization scheme. This was done keeping in mind the theories and theses of the study as well as the nature of the themes themselves.

I put all the fifty themes in ten different categories, for example, all the different themes on a new union were put in the category Union Creation. Appendix D explains these categories. The tables represent those broad categories rather than the original themes.

The themes

In most cases the Russian leaders talked about particular agreements or treaties. In a minority of cases they did talk about a particular visit, or negotiations in general, or all the different kinds of actions together. Table 6.1 contains the frequencies with which the broad themes were uttered by the Russian leaders. The first column of the table represents the categories of the themes, the second column contains the simple frequencies of the particular broad theme categories, the third column shows the percent for a particular theme category of all the occurrences of the ten theme categories. Thus 16% for Union Creation category in the third column and first row of Table 6.1 signifies that the theme occurred 16% of the times the total ten categories occurred.

Table 6.1
Themes appearing in Russian elites' statements

Theme Category	Frequency	% of Total
Union Creation	28	16
Link Preservation	21	12
Future Link	27	16
Defence	3	2
Ethnic Issues	17	10
Uncertainty	22	13
Comparison	30	17
Sovereignty	15	9
Identification	3	2
Neutral	7	4
Total	173	101

Table 6.2 gives the simple frequencies of the categories for each year. Since less statements were available for 1991 the total frequencies for 1991 are less. There were other reasons for the distribution as well. Tables 6.3, 6.4, 6.5 show the distribution by republics. Some utterances were republic specific some were general -- about the process or some components thereof. The second column of Table 6.5 contains themes that were not republic

specific. I put all three Baltic republics into the same category because their politics was similar and they received almost the same treatment from Russia.

Table 6.2
Themes uttered in 1990 and 1991

Theme Category	June-Dec. 90	Jan.-Aug. 91
Union Creation	20	8
Link Preservation	15	6
Future Link	15	12
Defence	2	1
Ethnic Issues	6	11
Uncertainty	16	6
Comparison	18	12
Sovereignty	7	8
Identification	1	2
Neutral	2	5
Total	102	71

The first four theme categories are the linkage themes which dominate Table 6.1 in terms of the number of times they occurred. These are the themes which paint a picture of the cooperation process as a linkage preservation or linkage creation mechanism. As a single theme the Comparison theme has the highest frequency. Very often the Russian elites compared their actions to the way the central government was handling things. The characterization of the process often was comparative. The impression that the RSFSR government was trying to impose control on a chaotic and uncertain situation was conveyed quite often, twenty two times. The Ethnic Issue theme was uttered less frequently than expected, only sixteen times. A similar situation prevailed as regards affirmation of sovereignty of the republics. The rest of the themes occurred with very low frequency.

The signing of treaties and agreements and protocols, the visits, and all the activities together will somehow lead to a different kind of Union --

this was a dominant theme. This was the Union Creation theme. It was part of the four linkage themes and the most important linkage theme. This theme had two aspects: character related, procedural. Sometimes the speakers talked about what kind of a Union was being created, at others, how this Union was being created and should be created. Again and again it was made clear that Russia did not want the Union to simply disappear. Its activities were not leading to that end.

Table 6.3
Distribution of themes by republics

Theme Category	Belarus	Ukraine	Kazakhstan
Union Creation	2	3	1
Link Preservation	2	3	2
Future Link	0	4	2
Defence	0	0	0
Ethnic	0	1	0
Uncertainty	1	6	6
Comparison	4	4	1
Sovereignty	1	3	0
Identification	0	0	0
Neutral	1	0	0

Sometimes it was not made clear what kind of a Union was going to be created as when Silaev said when he came to sign the economic agreement with Kyrgyzstan that the signing of agreements was constructing the Union or giving the Union a second life.[6] Yeltsin told the RSFSR Supreme Soviet that the Treaty On the Bases of Inter-State Relations between the RSFSR and Ukraine was the opportunity for establishing a community of sovereign states. But a number of times the nature of the future Union was clearly delineated. It was going to be an economic Union. Silaev once simply asserted that it was necessary to create an economic Union. This was because after the Union parliament rejected the Shatalin-Yavlinsky Plan Russia needed to do something.[7] But before that he once said in an interview that serious processes of disintegration had started and it was not due to Russia's fault.

92 Inter-republican cooperation

Russia could not allow the profound links among the republics to melt away. So it was trying to hold on to these ties by creating an economic Union on the basis of economic advantages. Granberg once said that the Russian government wanted to build a unified market economy. This theme in his speech was followed by the thoughts that the Union Treaty was the priority before but not any longer. Now problems had to be solved in much more difficult conditions. This implied that the economic Union was now the best way to go.[8] Although the nature of the Union was specified a number of times as the economic Union, frequently it was left vague without any explanations.

Table 6.4
Distribution of themes by republics

Theme Category	Moldova	Kyrgyzstan	Armenia
Union Creation	0	5	1
Link Preservation	2	3	0
Future Link	1	5	3
Defence	0	0	0
Ethnic Issues	2	2	0
Uncertainty	0	1	0
Comparison	5	8	1
Sovereignty	0	4	0
Identification	0	0	0
Neutral	0	0	0

More has been said about the procedure of creating a Union than the nature of the Union. The core treaties and even the less important agreements were forming the basis of the new Union. The procedural ideas displayed mutations over time. The first time the procedural aspect was revealed was in early August 1990 when Yeltsin spoke to the Latvian parliament. He described the proposed Latvian-Russian Treaty on the Bases of Inter-State Relations as getting to a common position about the fate of the Union. By the end of November the treaty signing process had become facilitating the signing of the Union Treaty because they would be the basis thereof and they were stabilizing the situation in the country so the Union

Table 6.5
Distribution of themes by republics

Theme Category	Baltic States	General
Union Creation	4	12
Link Preservation	1	8
Future Link	6	6
Defence	0	3
Ethnic Issues	10	2
Uncertainty	2	6
Comparison	3	4
Sovereignty	4	3
Identification	2	1
Neutral	5	1

Treaty could be signed.[9] When in December 1990, the Treaty on the Bases of Inter-State Relations was signed with Belarus, the procedural strategy was made crystal clear. First there would be bilateral treaties among the big republics then a quadrilateral treaty then the other republics could join it.[10] After the attacks on the Lithuanian radio and television tower, Russia began to talk about an agreement to form a Union among Belarus, Kazakhstan, Russia, Ukraine and Uzbekistan. Nobody could now sit around waiting for the Union Treaty to be signed. But in July when agreement had been reached with Gorbachev on the Union Treaty to be signed in August, 1991, Yeltsin referred to the agreements and the core treaty signed with Kyrgyzstan as the reliable basis for the Union Treaty.

As Table 6.2 demonstrates the Union Creation Theme occurred most in 1990. We have seen on the procedural aspect of the matter, the Russian position was revealed to be quite mature by the end of December 1990.

The Link Preservation theme is so called because it contained thoughts that Russia's interactions were promoting continuity rather than a breach with the past. These ideas were expressed in three ways: assertive, defensive, and credit taking. Most of the times Russia asserted that the treaties or agreements signified a transition to horizontal relations. Relations had been conducted through vertical links before but now relations would be conducted directly. These themes are continuity themes because they do not envisage qualitatively new ties but conducting the same relations only directly by the republics themselves. The use of the term horizontal rather than bilateral of course presupposes continuity within a larger structure. In a defensive mode of expression, Silaev once said that signing of bilateral treaties was not breakup of the Union and the linkages it signified.[11] Such statements were made to respond to accusations in the hard-line newspapers that Russia was trying to break-up the Union. The Russian officials not only defensively stated that they were not breaking up the Union but tried to take credit for doing something which no one else could do. They pointed out that when the vertical ties were collapsing, these inter-governmental agreements would help preserve them as well as strengthen them.[12] This strengthening and improving would be of the existing multifaceted ties. Such statements do not anticipate future uncertainty in relations because the republics would become sovereign or independent states.

The Future Linkage themes are different from preservation themes in that it is not clear that continuation is meant rather than more ties in the future between two entities that were sovereign. I have included in this category the thoughts that a particular treaty was going to lead to many more agreements between the parties on all aspects of relations. This was simply a statement which foresaw ties in the future. Sometimes they said that the talks would lead to political, economic, and cultural relations. In Ukraine's case these future relations were going to be good neighbourly relations.[13] Granberg's comment that cooperation would lead to a complex of all different types of relations was typical (Zharkov, August 3, 1990, p. 3). It was said there would be cooperation in foreign relations, coordination in every aspect of economic activities (Kozyrev, December 22, 1990, p. 3). It is true that describing and evaluating the same process as continuation of relations as well as future relations sound contradictory. Since the process itself was blending contradictory elements -- holding back and letting go -- it was only natural that it was being referred to using seemingly irreconcilable concepts.

The last of the four linkage category is Defence. Defence was referred to only three times. Although they are very few in number they show how seriously the RSFSR leadership was thinking about their alternative vision of the Union. Yeltsin and Kozyrev are the only officials who talked about the defence aspect of Russia's interaction with the other republics. They touched upon the place of the army and defence as a whole. Kozyrev wrote in his article that the collective security system that was being stipulated by the bilateral treaties would determine the place of the army in the community of sovereign states. Yeltsin, while talking about how the agreement among Belarus, Kazakhstan, Russia, Ukraine, and Uzbekistan was going to lead to a Union said the place of the army would be determined on a contractual basis. Considering the whole defence problem, Kozyrev said that the country was moving to a collective security system through the treaties.

Themes of uncertainty and chaos in the environment and fear of insecurity permeate the statements and speeches of the Russian leaders. The category Uncertainty covers them. The RSFSR officials talked about different kinds of threats coming from the political environment surrounding them. One of those themes was that because the republics had declared sovereignty the old way of conducting affairs had become hopelessly outdated. The old Union with some changes would not do. So Russia was establishing brotherly relations with a sovereign partner.[14] In his speech to the Russian parliament on the Russian Ukrainian Treaty on the Bases of Inter-State Relations Yeltsin said that the objective conditions were such that the republics after declaring sovereignty could not remain trapped in the old vertical relations. A more practical point was raised by Shelov-Kovedyaev when he said that the republics could not simply declare sovereignty and claim whatever was on their territory as rightfully theirs. The economic agreements allowed for negotiations on those thorny economic issues. A sense of economic crisis underway for some time had been cited as reasons why both economic agreements and core inter-state treaties had to be signed. The economy was disintegrating, it was in a state of serious crisis and in need of stabilization. The agreements would stabilize the economic situation.[15] About the major treaty between Belarus and Russia, Kozyrev said that it was an opportunity to resolve the economic crisis together. And also the economy had to be stabilized before the Union Treaty could be signed.

But more frequently than the economic disintegration the fear of uncoordinated economic reform was raised. Closely related to the economic disintegration were the economic dislocations and problems resulting from the reform efforts of all the republics. If such efforts were to be carried out in isolation or without coordination there would be many negative effects so the republics including Russia needed to cooperate to synchronize reforms with the purpose to have a smooth transition to a market economy.

Along with these economic insecurities fear of ethnic conflicts was mentioned as well. Referring to Baltic-Russian cooperation and Georgian-Russian interactions, Khasbulatov said that those were needed to eliminate the likelihood of serious ethnic conflicts.[16] Yeltsin told the Russian Supreme Soviet that he had gone to Estonia after the attacks on Lithuania because he wanted to prevent ethnic conflicts.

Comparing Russian actions to what was happening, to the reality of the Soviet system, and to the past in general was the way to characterize any particular cooperative action or cooperation in general. The category Comparison in Table 6.1 captures these themes and has the highest frequency as a single category. Very often Russian leaders referred to their own orientation towards the republics as departure from tradition. This was turning a new leaf in the history of relations of Russia and its partner. The Soviet system was a super-centralized system, and inter-republican cooperation was going to destroy that centralized political and economic system. It was a more efficient way to solve practical problems whereas the Soviet way was the encumbered bureaucratic way. There were clear comparisons as when the interactions were characterized as completely new, and getting rid of the old, out-dated system. There were implicit comparisons when it was implied that horizontal relations would help the republics develop and develop quickly and become capable of providing their people with a high standard of living. The following was implied, the central government's policies were not going to do that because it was clinging to socialism and vertical relations trying to convince the republics with some cosmetic legislative changes.[17]

Comparison was done to attract the republics to the Russian side. Demonstrating the efficiency and moral superiority of the Russian policy to the general public also worked behind it. Comparison was often done through characterization of the whole process or a single agreement as something novel. Such definition permits use of sweeping terminology, thus efforts to propagandize cannot be ruled out.

Rights of the Russian speaking population in other republics were something which the RSFSR government wanted to secure. The themes on the ethnic issues are denoted by the category Ethnic Issues and has a fairly high frequency. The treaties on the Bases of Inter-State Relations were the means for conducting inter-state relations on the issue of minority rights in a civilized manner, on the basis of international norms. The policy of threats and tension would be counter productive. Sometimes the treaties were referred to as 'mandates' or 'opportunities' to exert influence on the republican policies on minority relations. But yet, one thing about the ethnic issue themes that has to be taken into consideration is that this theme came up again and again in relation to the Baltic states (see Table 6.5). In case of Belarus it did not come up. Because of the Baltic states' efforts to make it harder to become citizens there were concerns about the Russians living in those republics. And, as the next chapter will demonstrate, Russian acceptance of formal independence of the Baltic states also prompted the Russian government to be more careful.[18]

Thoughts that affirmed republican sovereignty occurred with much fewer frequency than the linkage themes. Table 6.1 shows that pronouncements that could be classified as supportive of the claims of the republics to sovereignty occurred fifteen times. Sometimes the RSFSR leaders said directly that the treaty in question or Russia's new relations with the republics were realization of the declaration of sovereignty of the republics. At others, equality among partners was stressed; the Kyrgyz-Russian treaty was described as exemplifying equal partnership between the two peoples.[19]

The frequency for the other two categories, Identification and Neutral, are very low. But one significant point about the neutral themes -- themes which did not indicate whether Russia was seeing the republic as an entity inside a future Union or as a completely independent state -- occurred most of the times when Russian leaders were referring to their relations with the Baltic republics, the republics which Russia was willing to accept as independent.

The units (sampling units) for 1991 were less in number than the ones selected for 1990. Nevertheless, I obtained the distribution of the themes over the two years. This was done primarily to get an idea of what themes were uttered in 1990. As Table 6.2 demonstrates majorities of the linkage themes occurred in 1990. So did the uncertainty and comparison themes. This of course jibes with the events data analysis done in chapter three. The RSFSR had a well thought out policy of cooperation when the government was formed; it did not become mature in 1991 when outside observers had started to have misgivings about the viability of the Soviet state. As a matter of fact 1990 witnessed the signing of the most important treaties between Russia and Ukraine, Russia and Belarus, and Russia and Kazakhstan. Consequently, the themes of uncertainty in the environment decreased in the Russian leaders' speeches.

Tables 6.3, 6.4 and 6.5 give the distribution of the themes by republics. The category general in Table 6.5 indicates themes which did not refer to relations with any particular republics but dealt with the phenomenon in general terms. Armenia is the republic in Table 6.4 with which a Treaty on the Bases of Inter-State Relations had not been signed. The rest of the republics signed such treaties. I put the Baltic republics in the same category. There is very little republic-wise variation in the themes. The republics other than Armenia show similar distributions. The small variation happened because of the variation in the number of statements themselves and the frequency of a particular category. In case of the Baltic states the Ethnic Issue themes and Neutral themes occurred more and this has already been pointed out. Such a distribution by republics underscores two points. First, there was very little audience specificity in the statements; second, the same themes were uttered in different republics because the RSFSR leadership wanted to emphasize the same objectives: creation of an alternative Union, bilateral ties, and Russian flexibility as opposed to central rigidity.

Some general characteristics of the themes

If we look at the data as a whole they display some features which needs to be discussed at some length. The major ones are: contradiction, lack of change over time, the tendency to generalize, difference between Russian leaders' pronouncements and those of the leaders of their partner republics, almost no rank ordering of theme, leaving out certain features.

The contradictory nature of the themes has already been hinted at. The Russian officials made statements like they were destroying the existing structure of relations and at the same time continuing the historical ties. These were new relations and at the same time continuity of old linkages.

The data do not show much time sensitivity in the sense there is no significant change in the data over time. Except in a very few cases, e.g., Union Creation (procedural aspect), Uncertainty, Ethnic Issue, and Neutral themes, there is hardly any change from 1990 to 1991. Especially significant is the fact that most of the Union Creation themes occurred in 1990. This is indicative of the fact that from the very beginning the idea of the alternative Union was at the root of Russian thinking.

There was a pronounced tendency to generalize about the cooperation as a whole. Russian leaders, when speaking about Russia's relations, with another republic, or about a particular treaty, tended to generalize about the whole process. They did not simply talk about the particular treaty but all the treaties Russia was signing. They preferred to emphasize how the republics, which included Russia, were building the new Union from below rather than Russia and Kyrgyzstan doing that. This tendency becomes more striking when the generalization occurs in the context of such limited purpose agreements such as the economic agreements the declared purpose for signing which was to ensure 1990 level supply in 1991. This is what Silaev did in October, 1990, when he talked about preserving the Union while discussing the economic agreement with Kyrgyzstan.

There were significant differences in the themes raised by the Russian leaders and the ones stressed by the leaders of its partners. The leaders of Russia's partner republics stressed the fact that signing treaties and conducting bilateral relations through such treaties were equivalent to marching down the road of sovereignty almost always when they spoke. The

Ukrainian leader, Leonid Kravchuk, stressed the fact, after signing the Treaty on the Bases of Inter-State Relations, that this was a treaty between two equal sovereign partners. The republican leaders also stressed the utilitarian aspect of such cooperation rather than the longstanding ties between the partners or continuation thereof. They said the treaty was based on mutual advantages and economic benefits would ensue from it. One theme that did not occur in the statements of the republican leaders was that there would be numerous agreements on all different aspects of relations after the particular treaty. Especially interesting was the speech delivered by Ashkar Akayev when Yeltsin was visiting Kyrgyzstan. He said that the Union to be formed must be the Union of the real independent (nezavisimye) states, real equal states. He reminded Russia of Russian imperialism before the Soviet period started, especially the Kyrgyz uprising of 1916. The word 'independence (nezavisimost')' was a term Yeltsin never used in his speeches in Kyrgyzstan, he kept using the term 'sovereignty (suverenitet)'. Indeed he used 'independent' a very few times and only in 1990. The Russian leaders' effort was to portray the Soviet period as negative not the pre-Soviet Russian era. As a matter of fact, Yeltsin reminded the Ukrainians about Russian-Ukrainian unity against foreign attacks in the long gone past of the pre-Soviet period.

While going through the statements of the RSFSR elites I did not perceive any deliberate rank ordering of themes. Sometimes the economic issues came first, at others the renewal of the Union. The use of the comparative or superlative degrees was kept at a minimum. When used there was no consistency in applying them to only one issue. For example, about twice the minority rights aspect of the treaties were described as the most important aspect, but that was done again, at least once each, while referring to the Union Creation function and economic linkages in the treaties.

Some aspects of relations dealt with in the Treaties on the Bases of Inter-State Relations were hardly talked about. As we shall see in chapter seven next, each one of these treaties dealt with security and foreign relations aspects. While talking about these treaties Russian officials hardly raised the security or defence aspect and almost never foreign relations aspect. These were the harsher sides of these treaties and more clearly demonstrate how far Russia had gone in challenging the centre. If they were uttered to the republican audiences the charm of the treaties as destroyer of the old Soviet framework of relations would have been eroded.

Conclusion

A comprehensive set of statements and speeches of RSFSR elites were content analysed to find out what these leaders thought they were doing through the web of relations they were creating between Russia and the other Union republics. Posing a number of questions, I tried to get different dimensions of the thinking of the Russian officials.

These leaders made it clear that Russia was not for the breakup of the Soviet Union. Russia was really rejuvenating the Union in a better way. This Union was sometimes described as an economic Union, at others only as the Union. This future Union was talked about only in vague and positive terms. If themes of continuity and future links are combined with the themes of Union Creation, then Russian leaders were saying that their relations with the republics during this particular period aimed at retaining and creating a nexus of linkages. The strong emphasis on the Union and coordination of economic reform negates one assumption in the book. I assumed at the beginning that Russia was safeguarding imperial interests by tying up the republics through bilateral linkages, but the analysis here demonstrates that it was not only bilateral linkages but also the framework of a Union -- multilateral linkages.

There was a sense of insecurity among the Russian elites. They felt the economic situation was getting out of control. The republics had created a new situation by declaring sovereignty which required an innovative approach. There could be ethnic conflicts if the situation was not handled properly. Thus they conveyed the sense that they felt the need to control the situation. Their inter-republican cooperation was such a controlling mechanism.

There was frequent comparison between Russian policy and what was and what had been in the Soviet Union. This cast Russia in a favourable light. It drew out the differences between the more efficient, and more practical ways of the Russian leadership and the inflexibility of the central leadership.

The validity of the method used is confirmed by the results in the preceding chapters. Those results are not contradicted by the explanations given by RSFSR leaders of their actions. The only difference is, the preceding chapters did not lay emphasis on renewal of the Union in the form that is indicated by the statements. The fact that Russia viewed its cooperation would serve as the basis of the Union Treaty and only as transition to horizontal relations not those between independent states show that Russia wanted to renew the Union with not too many changes. In other words, it was not going to be the benign Union of completely independent states like the European Community or the British Commonwealth. The next chapter confirms the findings of the content analysis indicating that the Russian effort was to minimize uncertainty by proceeding to create a multilateral entity, a Union, as well as generating numerous bilateral ties.

It has hypothesis validity because the data have behaved the way predicted by the theoretical orientation and the theses informing the study. The only difference is the Russian approach was narrower than I took it to be while articulating and expanding on the theses.

Notes

1. For a description of different kinds of validity tests see, Weber, Robert (1985), *Basic Content Analysis*, Sage Publications, Beverly Hills, pp. 18-21.

2. To avoid confusion, I will use the term 'Sampling unit' within parentheses, to indicate the unit being referred to contains the recording unit, despite the fact that probability sampling was not used to select the units.

3. For a content analysis using such a comprehensive set see Frost, Howard (1989), 'A Content Analysis of Recent Soviet Party-Military Relations', *American Journal of Political Science*, vol. 33, no. 1, pp. 91-136.

4. As examples of theme analysis in political science see, Breslauer, George (1984), 'Is there a Generations Gap in the Soviet Political Establishment: Demand Articulation by RSFSR Provincial Party First Secretaries', *Soviet Studies*, vol. 36, no. 1, pp. 1-25; Stewart, Philip, Blough, Roger, Warhola, James (1984), 'Soviet Regions and Economic Priorities: A Study in Politburo Perceptions', *Soviet Union*, 11, part 1, pp. 1-30.

5. For this mode of analysis see, Krippendorf, Klaus (1980), *Content Analysis: An Introduction to its Methodology*, Sage Publications, Beverly Hills, pp. 79-80.

6. *Moscow Television Service* (October 10, 1990), 'Silaev Interviewed for Republic Agreements'; translated in *FBIS* (October 12, 1990), pp. 109-110.

7. *Rossiiskaya gazeta* (December 5, 1990), 'Doklad I.S. Silaeva', p. 1.

8. *Ekho Litvy* (August 30, 1990), 'Alexander Granberg: Nas Obe"diniaet ideya obshchego rynka', p. 2.

9. *Rossiiskaya gazeta* (December 7, 1990), 'Vystuplenie B.N. Yeltsina pered slushateliami, prepodovateliami voennoi akademii im. F.E. Dzerzhinskogo',

p. 1.

10. See Silaev's statement in *Rossiiskaya gazeta* (December 21, 1990), 'Belorussiya-Rossiya: Dogovor podpisan', p. 2. In this same report Kozyrev also talked around the same theme.

11. Ibid.

12. *Kazakhstanskaya pravda* (October 31, 1990), 'Na vzaimovygodnoi osnove', p. 1.

13. *Pravda Ukrainy* (November 21, 1990), 'Razvivat' dobrososedskie otnosheniya mezhdu respublikami', pp. 1, 2.

14. Ibid.

15. *Kazakhstanskaya pravda* (November 23, 1990), 'Podpisan dogovor mezhdu Kazakhstanom i Rossiei', p. 1.

16. *TASS* (July 28, 1990), 'RSFSR's Khasbulatov on Talks with Lithuania'; translated in *FBIS* (August 1, 1990), pp. 58-9. Also see *Literaturnaya gazeta* (June 5, 1991), 'Khasbulatov on Elections, Reform Efforts', pp. 1-2; translated in *FBIS* (June 11, 1991), pp. 86-91.

17. For some comparison themes see *Moldova Suverana* (September 29, 1990), 'Yeltsin Discusses RSFSR-Moldova Treaty', p. 4, translated in *FBIS* (October 24, 1990), pp. 96-7; *Rossiiskaya gazeta* (December 28, 1990), 'K vozrozhdeniyu -- vmeste', p. 1; *Rossiiskaya gazeta* (February 2, 1991), 'Ob itogakh ekonomicheskogo i sotsial'nogo razvitia RSFSR v 1990 godu, funktsionirovanii ekonomiki respubliki, biudzhete RSFSR i tsenovoi politike v tekushchem godu: Doklad Predsedatelia Soveta Ministrov RSFSR I.S. Silaeva', pp. 1-2.

18. For thoughts on rights of the Russian minorities in the other republics see *Ekho Litvy* (August 30, 1990), 'Aleksandr Granberg: nas obe"diniyaet ideya obshchego rynka', p. 2; *Rossiiskaya gazeta* (January 15, 1991), 'Press konferentsiya predsedatelia Verkhovnogo Soveta RSFSR', p. 2; *Rossiiskaya gazeta* (January 22, 1991), 'O politicheskom polozhenii v RSFSR: vystuplenie B.N. Yel'tsina na III sessii Verkhovnogo Soveta RSFSR', p. 1; *Ekho Litvy* (August 1, 1991), 'Rech' Borisa Yel'tsina', pp. 1, 2.

19. *Sovetskaya Belorussiya* (October 21, 1990), 'Rossiya-Belorussiya: Ect' prochnyi most', p. 1; *Slovo Kyrgyzstana* (July 23, 1991), 'Bratia na vse vremena', pp. 1, 2.

7 Russian Treaties: The Interplay of Multilateral and Bilateral Relations

Introduction

As Bilder has stressed, in any cooperative relation the most important elements are the written agreements which the states have concluded (Bilder, 1981). This is also true in the Russian case. Among Russia's aggregate cooperative actions, we have seen in chapter three, the various written agreements constituted a significant portion. These treaties and agreements as they were called by the participants following their own legal traditions were the more concrete elements in the process because they were in black and white and often marked the culmination of other cooperative actions such as meetings and negotiation sessions.

More important than the fact that they were tangible documents, most of them drew the frameworks within which Russia's future relations with its partners were to operate. This is why these agreements are so important even in isolation from the whole cooperation process. They were drawn out as future determinants of Russia's relations with the union republics. We have so far taken a cursory look at the nature of these agreements and noted their major features with some references to the negotiation process. In this final chapter we will take a closer look at the agreements Russia signed with the other republics in the period under study.

The RSFSR signed different kinds of agreements with the constituent republics of the Soviet Union. Some of them were cultural, some economic, some on coordinating foreign relations of the republics with those of Russia, and some were on basic principles of inter-state relations. The cultural agreements were about facilitating cultural relations, the economic ones typically dealt with maintenance of supplies. The most important agreements were the ones which dealt with the bases of inter-state relations. They were so because they chalked out the nature of relations between the signing parties. They also formed the source of later agreements. These treaties are the focus of this chapter.

There are important reasons for narrowing the focus of the study to an analysis of these core treaties. These treaties were the basic and fundamental ones. The others either emanated from them or were peripheral because they dealt with much less important issues as stop gap measures. Being the core of the set of written agreements they would better capture the attitudes of the Russian policy makers. Other agreements will be drawn upon in the process of analysis as supplementary evidence. The other reason relates to the issue of feasibility. Treaties are special legal documents interpretation of which is governed by particular rules developed by international legal scholars and the Vienna Convention on the Laws of Treaties, 1969. Their analysis thus prove to be detailed, complex and laborious, making it often impossible to manage the analysis of one or a few treaties at a time.

Some facts about the treaties

Russia signed at least forty agreements and treaties with the republics. In classifying these agreements Russia followed the Soviet legal tradition. Agreements were those documents which dealt with less important issues and were typically signed by the members of the Council of Ministers depending upon the nature of the agreements. The education agreement with Armenia, for instance, was signed by the deputy education minister and the economic agreements were signed by Prime Minister Silaev. The agreements on the principles of inter-state relations were signed by the chair of the Supreme Soviet and after the June 1991 RSFSR presidential election, the president. The same was true of the former Soviet Union where less important agreements were called agreements and signed by ministers and peace treaties or treaties of friendship were signed by the chair of the Presidium of the Supreme Soviet (Triska and Slusser, 1962, chapter 3). Thus they classified their agreements according to the nature of the agreements as well as the treaty making authority.

Eight treaties on the bases of inter-state relations were signed with the following republics: Belarus, Estonia, Kazakhstan, Kyrgyzstan, Latvia, Lithuania, Moldova, and Ukraine. The treaties provided for ratification.

Unfortunately it is harder to determine whether a treaty was ratified or not than whether it was signed. This happens partly because the media consider the signing more newsworthy than ratification. It is the aviation agreements information on the ratification of which is easy to locate because the relevant UN agency keeps the records of ratification. The treaties with Belarus, Kazakhstan, and Ukraine were promptly ratified by the Russian Supreme Soviet. But it is not certain whether the other treaties were ratified. It is not unusual for states to take a number of years to ratify a particular treaty; Poland took three years to ratify its agreement with the Soviet Union on the legal standing of the Soviet trade delegation (Triska and Slusser, 1962, p. 300).

It is best to assume that the RSFSR concluded the rest of the treaties with the intention to ratify them. As a matter of fact, in the Protocol establishing diplomatic relations between Latvia and Russia the two parties pledged to conduct bilateral relations on the basis of, among other documents like the UN Charter, the yet to be ratified treaty on the bases of inter-state relations between Latvia and Russia.[1] None of the ratified treaties has been terminated invoking the *clasula rebus sic stantibus* or the change of conditions doctrine which nations can cite to terminate or renegotiate a treaty if fundamental changes have taken place.[2]

I have selected seven of the eight treaties for study. These are the ones Russia signed with the three Baltic republics and Belarus, Kazakhstan, Kyrgyzstan, and Ukraine. These treaties represent different geographic areas: the Baltic, the European (Slavic), and Central Asian republics. In addition, they mark different time points in the cooperation process. The treaties with Belarus, Kazakhstan and Ukraine were signed around the same time -- the end of 1990. The treaties with Estonia and Latvia were signed in January 1991. But the two treaties with Kyrgyzstan and Lithuania were concluded in July 1991.

These treaties do not have any protocols or annexes attached to them, therefore, the texts of the treaties themselves are objects of analysis. The authentic texts of each treaty are in two languages, one in Russian, the other in the language of the other treaty signing party, Ukrainian in the case of the Russian-Ukrainian treaty. No single language version has been preferred for any particular section of any treaty. Since this study is analysing Russian orientations the Russian texts will be used.

The mode of analysis

Any analysis involving treaties or agreements has the treaties and interpretation thereof as the centrepiece. This study will be no exception. This chapter is an effort to understand Russian attitudes as reflected in the most important treaties. These treaties by themselves cannot provide support for the theses that Russia was trying to weaken the Gorbachev government as well as salvage imperial interests. They have to be viewed in the context of all the different cooperative activities and the statements made by the Russian leaders.[3] As publicists in international law would be quick to point out, the treaty texts by themselves, in many cases, do not explain the treaties themselves.

Analysis of treaties are rarely done in political science. It falls within the purview of international law. However, a few studies have been conducted: one by Perez-Lopez (1979) on Cuban international relations which is primarily descriptive; Zafar Imam's (1983) study of Soviet friendship treaties with the Third World countries looks into the timing, locations of treaty partners, and some provisions of the treaties to make generalizations about treaty making behaviour of the USSR. There have been quantitative studies of issues dealt with by treaties with the aim to determine the nature of relations among countries (Shinobu, 1987). Such studies are of limited help in understanding provisions stipulated in treaties and what repercussions they can have in bilateral relations in the future because they study the treaties in terms of the issues covered, the number of treaties signed, the times the treaties were signed, and the kinds of partners with whom they were signed. This is why I shall rely on the principles of treaty interpretation that have been put forth in the writings on international law.

There exist mainly three modes of treaty interpretation: textual, subjective, and teleological. There are some ancillary principles which could be applied in any of these three modes of explanations.[4] The textual mode puts all the emphasis on the text and derives from Vattel's writings. This approach was the favoured one by international tribunals especially the Permanent Court of the League of Nations and the current International Court of Justice (ICJ) of the United Nations (UN). The Vienna Convention on the Laws of Treaties (Laws of Treaties) also favours the textual explanation. The assumption is, the text of the treaty should be read accepting the natural and normal meanings of the words and sentences relating them to the context. The context in this case is the whole treaty plus the annexes and protocols attached to it. Special meaning would be attached to words only if the parties originally intended them to have such meanings. Earlier, the Permanent Court emphasized the text so much that it stuck to a particular article of a treaty without putting it in the context of the whole treaty.[5]

International law scholars favouring the subjective approach have urged the necessity of going beyond the actual text of an agreement. This has been done largely for two reasons. First: the meaning of a treaty text is often not clear enough and cannot be interpreted properly without access to extratextual material such as the *travaux preparatoires* (the preparatory materials or negotiation documents) and subsequent application of the treaty by the parties. Second: many believe that an objective, textual interpretation of a treaty is what the treaty means to a third party rather than what the signers intended it to mean. This is why it is necessary to understand the meanings the signers assigned to different clauses, and articles. The *travaux preparatoires* are, therefore, indispensable -- they may contain 'defined' terms, 'explained' terms, or 'modified clauses'.[6] The Laws of Treaties deemphasize recourse to the *travaux* by making the method a supplementary means of interpretation.[7]

The teleological approach considers a treaty from the perspective of the goal it was supposed to achieve. When there is a dispute over an article of a treaty it will be explained in light of the goal the parties wanted to attain through this treaty. Multilateral conventions are often interpreted using the teleological approach, for instance, the ICJ has interpreted the UN Charter from this perspective. It is not unusual at all to interpret bilateral treaties from a teleological view. The ICJ used the teleological approach, as one of the approaches in deciding the *Saudi Arabia-Aramco Case* (McDougal, Lasswell, and Miller, 1967, pp. 170-1).

The ancillary principles which are often used do not constitute any major perspective of treaty interpretation. One example is the restrictiveness principle -- the rule according to which limits on the sovereignty of a state cannot be assumed but must be clearly set forth. The logical principle *expressio unius est exclusio alterius* is also used as one of such rules. This logical principle prescribes that whenever a given reference is expressly included in an agreement, all other related references must be considered as having been excluded. Tammelo (1967) has stressed that in understanding treaties, reliance should be on plausibility rather than on rules of formal logic. Very few logical principles are applied in treaty analysis as opposed to analysis of domestic laws.

The ICJ, taking the textual principle as its only approach has come over time to recognize and use the other principles all the time emphasizing the textual approach. Its decisions in various cases demonstrate that the other two modes of interpretation have been used. As McDougal et al (1967) point out, in some cases the ICJ has used all the approaches taking the four corners of the agreement or the text as its point of departure. These approaches then are not mutually exclusive. Principles of treaty interpretation are not hierarchically arranged.

This section of the analysis will be more dependent on the text of the treaties, the history of their signing and the statements made by Russian elites as discussed in the previous chapters. This is perfectly legitimate. Subsequent actions of the parties will be brought in whenever possible. References to other treaties will also be made. The *travaux preparatoires* will not be used because they are not available; states tend to hand them over to the courts only when there are disputes. Treaty analysis in academic writings have been done without them. I shall also focus on the main features of the treaties as stipulated in different sections rather than scrutinize every clause and phrase. The treaties were collected from the following sources: the Belarusian and Kazakh treaties from the *Vedomosti S"ezda Narodnykh Deputatov RSFSR i Verkhovnogo Soveta RSFSR* (January 14, 1991), Supreme Soviet of RSFSR, Moscow, pp. 113-16, and 117-20; the Estonian treaty from *Rossiiskaya gazeta* (January 17, 1991), p. 2; the Latvian treaty from *Rossiiskaya gazeta* (January 16, 1991), p. 1; the Lithuanian treaty from *Ekho Litvy* (July 31, 1991), pp. 1, 2; the Kyrgyz treaty from *Slovo Kyrgyzstana* (August 1, 1991), p. 2; and the Ukrainian treaty from *Pravda Ukrainy* (November 21, 1990), p. 1. The author will provide the texts of the treaties upon request. Although references to various articles of these treaties will be made throughout the chapter, the treaties themselves will not be repeatedly cited.

The treaties

It is true that all the seven treaties were signed to govern the nature of interstate relations between the parties, but all the seven treaties were not exactly the same. There are some differences between the treaty Russia signed with Ukraine and the three treaties it signed with Belarus, Kazakhstan, and Kyrgyzstan. There are significant differences between these four treaties taken together and the three treaties Russia signed with the Baltic states. Again, among the Baltic treaties, the treaty between Lithuania and Russia is different from the two Russia concluded with the other two Baltic states. This is why the first four treaties will be studied first and the Baltic treaties will be taken up later and analysed in terms of how they diverge from the non-Baltic treaties and what that signifies.

The first thing that strikes one about the treaties is their nature or scope. They have sweeping scopes, each one of them is very broad and deals specifically with every important aspect of bilateral relations. With the preambles eloquently setting the tone and frame of reference of the treaties, they tackle the issue of sovereignty and go on to specify the nature of relations in the spheres of foreign relations, defence, cultural and technical cooperation, future of the Union, economic relations, information exchange, communication and transport. The end of the treaties were devoted, as usually done, to dispute resolution, consultation, and ratification clauses.

Because of the nature and scope of the treaties, we are immediately faced with the question, why treaties of such broad range? Each one of the topics covered in these treaties could generate one major agreement, for instance, there could be a treaty on cooperation in the transport sector which could in turn generate a number of agreements on air transport, land transport, and river and sea transport, and finally transit through pipelines. Conversely, if Russia wanted to ascertain that the republics did not sever relations in a topsy turvy fashion, which was doubtful because that would have harmed the republics more, then general friendship treaties could be signed on the model of the Japanese-Ethiopian Treaty of friendship or the friendship treaty between Turkey and Jordan (TransJordan at the time).[8]

The Russian treaties are unusual in the sense that they do not resemble treaties between other countries of the same genre. They resemble more closely the treaties of friendship between the Soviet Union and some Third World countries, e.g. Afghanistan, Ethiopia, South Yemen, in their degree of vagueness and yet tenacity to encompass broad range of issues or aspects of bilateral relations.[9]

The similar nature of the treaties and the Russian leadership's repeated assertions to the effect that they wanted to sign such treaties first leave the distinct impression that there was a model treaty drafted by the Russian side and which was presented to the other party as the first step in negotiations. Countries, while negotiating the same kind of treaties, draft a model treaty which reflect their preferences. The United States has a model Bilateral Investment Treaty (BIT) which it presents to the other party as the point of departure for negotiations (Goodman, 1991). If this view is taken then the treaties with Belarus, Kazakhstan, and Kyrgyzstan come closest to the model.

The preambles

Preambles are useful tools in understanding treaties. They warn about the essence and directions of treaties. Many scholars have used the preambles as supporting evidence in explaining treaties.[10] Those who believe that a treaty contains no unnecessary phrases or parts subscribe to the view that preambles are important parts of treaties (McDougal, Lasswell, and Miller, 1967).

The preambles of the four treaties are unusually long. They assert that the treaties were ensuing from the declaration of sovereignty of each state. They were being concluded with the desire to build democratic states in each party's territories, wishing to further develop the historically close relations of the parties because that would serve the interests of the parties, supporting the reconstruction of the Union, affirming goals embodied in the UN Charter and the Helsinki Final Act and so forth. The preambles also contain the wish not to use any kind of force against one another.

The basic principles of the treaties are the declarations of independence of the parties. These declarations made each republic sovereign over its territory and people. The Union government did not accept the sovereignty of the republics. Russia found it acceptable to consider them sovereign. Thus the preambles serve notice that the signing parties were going beyond what was acceptable to the centre, Russia was going beyond. But there was another side to this part of the preambles. The treaties could conceivably proceed from other principles, such as those of self determination of nations or they could proceed from acceptance of the parties as subjects of international law.

The declarations of sovereignty of the republics were both liberating and constricting at the same time. None of the republics declared themselves independent but sovereign states.[11] The treaties were proceeding from a concept of limited sovereignty. This limited view of sovereignty is reflected in all the clauses of the preamble and some parts of the treaties themselves. The parties affirm their adherence to the principles and goals of the UN Charter and the Helsinki Final Act rather than accepting them both as determinants of behaviour. The UN Charter of course has a binding character but the Helsinki Act does not. They are put in the same category probably to underline the non-binding character of principles of documents.

The principle of non-use of force is put as a wish in the preamble rather than a categorical commitment embodied in an article. A serious non-use of force commitment has to be categorical and absolute (Czaplinski, 1992). There were other terms which could easily be substituted by stronger, more assertive of sovereignty, terms. With this weak meaning of sovereignty was combined the striving to renew the Union as a union of sovereign states. Thus the whole preambles convey the sense of sovereignty of states which have accepted a commitment to create a union. The preamble or any other section of the treaty with Ukraine does not contain a commitment to renew the Union, either on a voluntary basis as in the Belarusian treaty or just renew the Union as in the Kazakh Treaty. This happened because of Ukraine's stronger aspirations for sovereignty as compared to Kazakhstan or Belarus.

Recognition and borders

Closely related to the preambles are the articles on recognition and borders. The parties recognized each other as sovereign states and vowed not to engage in activities which would impinge upon the sovereignty of each other. They recognized each other's existing borders.

The recognition that mattered was not the recognition offered by the other republics, it was the recognition given by Russia. The wording of the clauses are imbued with a sense of reciprocity, yet they could be made far stronger from the perspective of the other republics and were made so in the Baltic treaties. Since these states did not exist as independent states the recognition was 'constitutive' rather than 'declaratory'.[12] As such they could be made firmer by recognition as subjects of international law and with defined borders. The recognition offered in the treaties is weak for another reason; one state can recognize the sovereignty of a state for the purpose of signing treaties but not necessarily as a person under international law. The United States offered such recognition to the Micronesian Islands, the US trust territories in the Pacific Ocean, for signing the Compact of Association with the United States (Armstrong, 1981, pp. 204-5).

But more important than the weak nature of recognition in these four treaties is the question why recognition was given in treaties which established bilateral relations on every conceivable level between the parties and contained promises to create an economic union. That recognition was offered within the framework of such a treaty made it conditional and part of a package deal. The Russian side's interpretation of the border clauses, as we shall see shortly, indicates that this was how Russia viewed it. Now and in the recent past recognition is not given in treaties. Recognition is offered through unilateral declarations, announcements, or diplomatic notes. Treaties were used farther in the past by Britain to recognize its former colonies. As the British-Jordanian treaty shows Britain retained extensive military facilities through the Annex to the treaty which recognized Jordan as an independent country.[13]

The conditional nature of these provisions are more pronounced in the clauses dealing with the borders. The republics recognized the existing borders. The vague term existing borders was used in the Belarusian (Article 2) and Kyrgyz (Article 6) treaties. The border clauses in the Kazakh (Article 6) and Ukrainian (Article 6) treaties were phrased more clearly. The borders of the latter two republics were recognized as the existing borders within the USSR. There were no annexes to the treaties delimiting the borders through lines in maps as the 1994 Israeli-Jordanian Treaty has.[14] There are no indications that border treaties would be signed later showing exactly where the borders would lie whereas important clauses of the treaties have always been accompanied by unequivocal commitments to sign agreements later. As a result the Russians do not accept the borders existing in the USSR (Bartnikas and Krutakov, 1994, p. 8). There also arose conflicting views regarding the Russian and Ukrainian borders.

After the Ukrainian Rada (parliament) declared independence following the failure of the August 1991, coup, to be effective after a referendum on December 1, 1991, the Russian president's press secretary, Pavel Voshchanov, promptly noted that Russia reserved the right to review the borders between itself and Ukraine in the case Ukraine became independent (Solchanyk, 1993). Ukraine was quick to refer to the 1990 treaty in which Russia and Ukraine recognized each other's borders. But the Russian side held the view that the borders were recognized in view of Ukraine's and Russia's existence within a future commonwealth-like entity (Solchanyk, 1993). The wording of the treaty and the purpose of the treaties as described by Russian leaders in their statements and as analysed in the preceding chapter will support the Russian interpretation more than the Ukrainian one although the vagueness of the clause provides Ukraine some leeway to stake its claim as it did. The Russian government held the same view about the borders of all the republics except the Baltic ones (Solchanyk, 1993, p. 347). It is only recently in 1994, that the Russian side decided to sign a border agreement with Ukraine (Orlov, June 17-23, 1994, p. 4). The fact remains that this instance of subsequent interpretation of the treaties by the Russian side underscores the conditional nature of the treaties.

Minority rights

Each of the treaties contain elaborate provisions on the rights of minority groups in the republics. We have seen in Chapter 5 that the Russian population was concerned about the fate of the Russians in other republics and it was reflected in questions asked during interviews of RSFSR leaders. They were very frequently asked questions about the Russians living outside the RSFSR. The Russian leaders themselves emphasized the fact that they were trying to legally defend the rights of the Russian minorities in other republics. They also saw the treaties as mandates for efforts to influence the other republics.

The minorities in each state would have the right to choose the citizenship of the state in which they were residing in conformity with the citizenship law of the concerned state. They would have all the rights, civil, political, economic and so on without being subject to any kind of discrimination. The list of rights was extensive indicating the effort not to exclude any rights so later those could be denied by a republic citing the *expressio unius est exclusio alterius* rule. The republics could defend the rights of their citizens in other republics and could provide all kinds of assistance. This very inclusive provision was followed by geographic rights. The geographic stipulation provided for the continued existence and protection of unique ethnic regions, apparently these areas are the Russian populated Eastern Ukraine, Russian majority Crimea, and almost exclusively Russian populated northern Kazakhstan.

Providing for the rights of minorities in treaties is not unusual. But what is striking about these treaties is the manner in which they were provided. The parties would be able to defend the rights of their people living in the territories of their treaty partners. The right to defend was not circumscribed by any provision thus it becomes a carte blanche. Coupled with the equivocal declaration renouncing the use of force this has an ominous ring. This is why analysts were quick to point out that Russian minorities would be an important reason for Russian intervention in these republics. Also the geographic rights given precluded any effort by the other states to settle their people in the particular unique ethnic formations. If Kazakhstan allowed any significant number of Kazakhs to settle in northern Kazakhstan it would be an infracture of the treaty.

Provisions giving minorities their rights can be limited by adding conditions and this was done in the German-Polish treaty of June, 1991. The treaty provided the German minority in Poland with their rights with the condition that Poland would respect those rights if they did not infringe upon her sovereignty and her obligations and rights under the UN Charter (Czaplinski, 1992).

Defence and foreign policy

Defence and foreign policy provisions have been worded to accommodate two kinds of relations. First: they deal with collective defence; second: they touch upon bilateral relations. The collective security provisions (Articles 7 of the Belarusian, Kazakh, and Ukrainian treaties) stipulated that the parties recognized the necessity of creating a collective security system. Articles 8 of these treaties provided for coordinated actions, among other spheres, in foreign policy. This coordination was to be realized through common institutions of the two parties. The Kyrgyz treaty did not have a collective security section. This was substituted with the provision (Article 7) that both the states recognized that defence would be ensured through the control of nuclear weapons by one Union authority. The variation in the Kyrgyz treaty was obviously because there had already been agreement that a Union Treaty would be signed.

The collective security provision and the foreign policy coordination clauses were vaguely and flexibly termed. The collective security articles have been drafted as parties recognizing the necessity of creating a collective security system and the foreign policy coordination clause was worded as parties having the basic principle that foreign policies would be coordinated. This is very vague wording. It was not clarified what kind of collective security system was envisaged. Nor was it specified whether foreign policy coordination would be done by bilateral institutions or multilateral institutions. The wording is flexible in the sense that they do not provide for unequivocal commitment to sign agreements on these issues. But they are not worded as general agreement to agree (agreement to agree) which would be very liberal (Bilder, 1981, pp. 34-6). Treaty provisions are worded vaguely for a number of reasons: either the parties could not agree on the particular issues so decided to leave them equivocally worded so both could interpret them the way they desired; the issues were peripheral to the main agreement so they clarified the central issues leaving the less important ones in the realm of 'agree to agree'; the parties had reached general agreement on the broad principles and simply decided to use general terms to state that.[15]

Recognizing that it was necessary to create a collective security system indicates a general agreement at the negotiation stage. The CIS Collective Security Council endorsed a draft agreement for a military alliance in July 1994. The agreement is about Russian nuclear protection of the other republics but also seeks to establish a collective security arrangement which, if attained, would amount to a Soviet type arrangement (Karatnycky, August 30, 1994, p. A13). Pursuit of such arrangements by Russia is permitted by the bilateral treaties. Ensuring bilateral and multilateral interaction could mean two things: a. defence would be multilateral and foreign policy coordination would be bilateral; b. defence would be collective, part of the foreign policy coordination would be bilateral, part of it multilateral. Russia probably did not mind if it was multilateral or bilateral so long as foreign policy was coordinated and the wording reflects that as well as giving the provisions the appearance of interactions among sovereign states. The subsequent behaviour of the parties indicate clearly the underlying general agreement about foreign policy coordination. Belarus and the RSFSR signed an agreement in April 1991 on cooperation in foreign economic policy. The agreement was signed to coordinate activities when joining multilateral economic fora like the IMF, World Bank, and GATT.[16]

The reverse of the defence and foreign policy coin was the article dealing with relations with the third party. The treaties took pain to make sure that there would be a provision dealing with foreign relations with the third party. Articles 16 of the Kazakh and Ukrainian treaties and Article 17 of the Belarus and Article 15 of the Kyrgyz treaty were about foreign relations with the third party or another country. On the face of it, these are very liberal and flexible provisions. They allow free interactions with other states and go so far as to let the parties sign collective security pacts.

This third party clause accentuates Russia's efforts to give the treaties the appearance of agreements between truly sovereign countries. No other article went so far to allow the states this much freedom. But these articles also constitute the glaring contradictions in otherwise consistent and unidimensional treaties. They have to be viewed in the context of the previous collective security stipulations and requirements to coordinate foreign policy. If these states were going to coordinate foreign policy with Russia they obviously could not interact with third parties without Russia having a say in that. Such contradictions in treaties are not unusual. In the Polish-US BIT, the United States was able to get Poland to agree to very liberal screening, production requirement, profit repatriation terms. But in the annexes to the treaty Poland negated much of what she had agreed to (Goodman, 1991).

Economic relations

All the four treaties have a general provision stipulating cooperation in different spheres, e.g., the economy, culture, and ecology. They also have lengthy articles on bilateral economic cooperation. There would be economic and technical cooperation on each level of activities: government level, municipal level, industry level, and individual level. The mechanism of economic cooperation would be figured out through later agreements. Cooperation in pricing policies was provided for.

More important than stipulations concerning bilateral cooperation is the agreement to cooperate in creating a common European and Eurasian market, in which sequence is not clarified but not hard to fathom. This article committed the signing parties to create an economic union. Again there was this combination of multilateral and bilateral ties. Both kinds of commitments if combined make for extremely close relations with Russia. It is clear that the republics themselves did not want to suddenly sever ties with Russia. Most of them also considered economic ties beneficial. But whether they would have made such sweeping commitments at the time is not clear at all. Ukraine's behaviour after the breakup of the Soviet Union attests to the contrary. It was not Russia but the other republics which scrambled to declare independence after the August 1991 coup. Even Kazakhstan did so although late in that year and later than the other Central Asian republics. We have to keep in mind that it took Russia till the end of 1994 to get all the republics to sign on to a payment union and agree to create a joint economic committee (Shermatova, October 28-November 3, 1994, p. 2). The clause on the development of a European market is unclear, to say the least. It could be interpreted as establishment of economic ties with Western European countries in coordination.

All these economic provisions were cemented by the pledge that none of the parties would do anything to damage the economy of the other. What would be considered damage was not specified. Kazakhstan's selling more petroleum could be considered damage, Ukraine's selling uranium could be considered damage.[17]

Dispute resolution and termination

Like any bilateral treaties between sovereign states the treaties under discussion contain dispute resolution sections. Nations usually use dispute management clauses as risk minimization tactics. Thus dispute resolution strategies are spelled out clearly. They are interconnected with the termination clauses. Most treaties designate the ICJ as the arbitration authority. Some treaties make it obligatory for a treaty partner to consider an issue, in good faith, within a reasonable period of time (60 days in case of some US treaties) once the other partner raises it. If the dispute is not taken up or reviewed through proper mechanism or cannot be resolved then the dissatisfied party can unilaterally terminate a treaty or withdraw from it if it is multilateral.

A third party like the ICJ is chosen in most bilateral treaties because the court is thought to have expertise and is neutral enough to give a balanced judgement. Third party arbitration limits losses by putting the burden on the parties to convince an impartial body with good enough evidence why one of them is right.

Articles 15 of the Kazakh and Ukrainian treaties, Article 16 of the Belarusian treaty, and Article 14 of the Kyrgyz treaty deal with dispute resolution. They ensure dispute resolution through bilateral negotiations. If a party does not take up the complaint of the aggrieved party nothing can be done. Such wording of the clause does not preclude referring the dispute to a third party but the omission of a third party can be interpreted as lack of enthusiasm for such dispute resolution mechanism as well. None of these four treaties provide for unilateral termination although change through mutual agreement is envisaged.

Treaties with the Baltic Republics

Russia's three treaties with the Baltic republics had important differences with the four treaties discussed above. Among the three Baltic treaties the treaty with Lithuania was different from those with Estonia and Latvia in that Lithuania was recognized more strongly as a sovereign state.

In the preambles and Articles 1 of the three treaties the three Baltic republics were recognized as sovereign states and full subjects of international law. They had the right to full state independence which none of the non-Baltic states had. Lithuania was able to get Russia to denounce the annex to the 1940 German-Soviet agreement through which the USSR obtained control over the Baltic states. Both Estonia and Latvia had, it was agreed, full legislative, executive, and judicial powers over their own territories (Articles 2), something that was not given to the non-Baltic states.

In the Estonian and Latvian treaties the signers pledged to respect the territorial integrity of one another and to sign treaties later delimiting the borders. The promise to sign a border treaty is not recognition of the existing border, granted that, border treaties are signed with foreign countries and once the borders are demarcated through treaties such treaties cannot be terminated citing the *clasula rebus sic stantibus*.

The Baltic treaties have especially elaborate provisions on the minority rights, particularly the Lithuanian treaty because of Lithuania's sterner orientation towards the citizenship issue. All the Baltic republics were strict about citizenship and contemplated introducing some qualifications requirement. At one point they even offered money, a paltry sum of a few thousand rubles, to the Russians who would leave their territory to resettle in Russia or their ethnic homelands. The Lithuanian treaty provided for coordinating migration policy and providing for resettlement. None of the treaties contain anything similar to protection of unique geographic regions despite the fact that this could be done in case of Estonia because a part of eastern Estonia is Russian populated. This happened because of Russia's willingness to recognize Estonia as an independent state as well as the tough negotiation tactics of the Estonians.[18]

Russia was more yielding in the area of foreign relations and defence with the Baltic republics. None of them made any commitment to join a collective security system with Russia. But they were effectively put in alliance relations with it. The treaty parties in the Baltic treaties obliged themselves at the very beginning of the treaties not to breach norms of international law or allow a third party to do so in relation to their treaty partners. Such a security clause obliges the Baltic states to come to Russia's aid in case there is hostility against it. The Lithuanian treaty went a little further (Article 2) in terms of flexibility permitting Lithuania to conduct its own foreign relations in the way she saw fit; she could enter a collective security system with other states. But here too the provision was circumscribed by a Lithuanian commitment to sign a treaty with Russia later on defence and security relations. Estonia and Latvia (Articles 9) were given the right to realize their sovereignty in the realms of defence and security but they would sign treaties with Russia defining cooperation in these spheres of state activities.

In addition to this informal alliance, each of the Baltic states is committed not to allow the formation of groups hostile to Russia and Russia, in turn, would not allow formation of groups hostile to the Baltic states. This is a section which exactly resembles such provisions from Soviet peace treaties with Eastern European countries (Triska and Slusser, 1962, p. 252). It sounds anachronistic with the demise of communism but apparently was put in as an added risk management tactic. Since the treaties were signed immediately after Soviet attacks on Lithuanian television and radio tower these were statements aimed at the central authorities as well.

The third party relations clauses are there in each of the Baltic treaties (Articles 19 of the Estonian and Latvian treaties and Article 16 of the Lithuanian treaty). But they are different from those in the non-Baltic treaties in a significant way. They do not give the Baltic states the right to join any other collective security system. Thus the Baltic states are not obliged to join a collective security system with Russia and its partners nor are they allowed to join any other collective security system by omission, while they are in an informal alliance relation with Russia.

Although the commitment to coordinate foreign relations including admission into multilateral fora were worded more vaguely they are there. In Lithuania's case (Article 8) the wording was more in Lithuania's favour because it was not a pledge to coordinate foreign relations but simply cooperate in different ways in foreign relations. The article was worded 'The high contracting parties consider it would be useful to cooperate', rather than 'The parties' basic position is that', as in the Belarusian treaty (Article 8).

The economic relations between the Baltic republics and Russia as specified in the treaties are similar to those laid down in the non-Baltic treaties with the exception of relations with Lithuania. Lithuania did not make a commitment to develop, together with Russia, an Eurasian economy and an all European economy. But she did pledge to integration together into the European economy indirectly when she promised to cooperate to facilitate integration of her economy and the Russian economy into the international economy (Article 15). The wording in the Baltic treaties are more flexible in this regard.

There were other important differences between Russia's Baltic and non-Baltic treaties. The transportation sections were different. The sections in the Baltic treaties carefully limited the provisions by allowing only goods and passenger carriers through one another's territories whereas such limits were absent in the other treaties thereby allowing transport of soldiers and military equipments by implication. The differences discussed above underscore the fact that the RSFSR was inclined to recognize the Baltic states as independent with close economic, political and cultural ties (the Baltic states were also committed to maintain intimate cultural ties with Russia).

Lithuania was treated better in the core treaty than any other republic in terms of wording. But that happened because Lithuania agreed to sign an agreement on the Kaliningrad oblast. This agreement committed Lithuania to help any way she could in the continuous development of the Kaliningrad oblast. Kaliningrad is an area which formally belonged to the RSFSR during the Soviet period, but is separated from it by Lithuania. Lithuania claimed this territory at least twice this century (Smith, 1992). It was historically known as 'little Lithuania', to the Lithuanians because of the ethnic Lithuanians living there. Yeltsin made it known to the Lithuanian government that the treaty on inter-state relations, a treaty that would recognize Lithuania as a state under international law, could not be signed unless there was an agreement on Kaliningrad. Lithuania finally agreed to sign the agreement on Kaliningrad recognizing it as an oblast of the RSFSR (Article 1 and the title of the agreement).[19] In this agreement Lithuania also agreed to sign an agreement later on transport of soldiers and military equipment to and from Kaliningrad. In exchange of the agreement on Kaliningrad, Lithuania was able to get more favourable wording in the core treaty.

Conclusion

The treaties analysed in this chapter formed the core of the treaties RSFSR elites signed with the other republics. The Russian government leaders wanted to sign these treaties first and they described them in their statements as the basis of a better, improved and more progressive union. With the exception of the Baltic treaties, the text of the treaties were in conformity with Russian desire to form a union around Russia.

The broad range of the treaties are revealing. Nations usually eschew signing on to such sweeping commitments as a risk reduction tactic. They prefer signing narrower treaties on different aspects of relations. By 1990, even in Belarus desire for independence was growing and all the republics were disillusioned with Gorbachev's reform efforts. No doubt most of them wanted good economic relations among themselves but it would be wrong to think they desired strong political, social, foreign relations ties with Russia that were stipulated in the treaties, Central Asian misgivings at the time of independence notwithstanding.

The treaties contain recognition of the republics as sovereign, but in the case of the non-Baltic states this sovereignty was not to mean complete sovereignty. The recognition of sovereignty within the framework of a broad treaty made it conditional, and that was how the Russian government felt or interpreted the treaties. At the beginning of the book I assumed that Russia was willing to recognize all the republics as having complete sovereignty and as subjects of international law. But the treaties allow for that only in the case of the Baltic republics. As regards the other republics Russia was not willing to travel that far a distance.

Juxtaposition of multilateral and bilateral relations in the same treaty seems to be a risk minimization effort and also indicative of Russia's feeling that once the republics were recognized as sovereign they might want to strengthen that sovereignty. That is exactly what happened when the republics, one after another, declared independence following the bungled August 1991 coup. Also creating a multilateral body might take time and then bilateral relations would prove useful linkages. Whatever was the thinking it is clear that every effort was made to keep the republics tied to Russia as subordinate actors.

It is true that Russia was ready to recognize the Baltic states as independent states, but even then the linkages between these states and the RSFSR were to be almost as strong as those between it and the non-Baltic states. Lithuania got better wording in its treaty with Russia because it signed the agreement on Kaliningrad. Even then, a Lithuanian observer remarked, after the Lithuanian-Russian treaty on the bases of inter-state relations were signed, that Russia recognized Lithuania 'obliquely'.

Russia went beyond Gorbachev by wanting to formally call the republics sovereign however limited that sovereignty was. The RSFSR government also recognized the republics' right to have the kind of property relations they wanted. Other than that the republics, with the feeble exception of the Baltic republics, were to revolve around Russia much like the olden days. This is strongly supportive of the assumptions from which the book proceeds, that Yeltsin's government in Russia wanted to weaken the communist government of the Soviet Union by supporting the demands for independence of the republics and at the same time safeguard the interests of the Russians which formed the core of an empire. The thrust of the treaties, specific provisions of the treaties, as well as the style of drafting of the treaties -- for example the use of the logical principle *expresso unius est exclusio alterius* in stipulating that there would be treaties on other aspects of relations not included in the present treaties -- are indicative of this.

Notes

1. For this protocol see, *Sbornik mezhdunarodnykh dogovorov SSSR i Rossiiskoi Federatsii* (1992),'Protocol ob ustanovlenie diplomaticheskikh otnoshenii mezhdu Rossiiskoi Sovetskoi Federativnoi Sotsialisticheskoi Respublikoi i Latviiskoi Respublikoi', vol. 47, Mezhdunarodnaya otnosheniya, Moscow, pp. 25-6.

2. For a discussion of this doctrine see, Nozari, Fairborz (1971), *Unequal Treaties in International Law*, S-Byran Sundt & Co, Stockholm, pp. 134-71.

3. Statements of treaty signing parties are important clues in understanding and interpreting treaties. See, McDougal, Myres, Lasswell, Harold, and Miller, James (1967), *The Interpretation of Agreements and World Public Order: Principles of Content and Procedures*, Yale University Press, New Haven.

4. This discussion on interpretation of treaties are based on the following sources, Tammelo, Iimer (1967), *Treaty Interpretation and Practical Reason: Towards a General Theory of Legal Interpretation*, The Law Book Company Ltd., Sydney, Australia; McDougal, Myres, Lasswell, Harold, Miller, James (1967), *The Interpretation of Agreements and World Public Order: Principles of Content and Procedures*, Yale University Press, New Haven; Vandevelde, Kenneth (1988), 'Treaty Interpretation from a Negotiator's Perspective',

Vanderbilt Journal of Transnational Law, vol. 21, no. 2, pp. 281-311; Shabatai, Rosenne (1989), *Developments in the Law of Treaties, 1945-1986*, Cambridge University Press, Cambridge, pp. 448-76.

5. See the Court's interpretation of article 3 of the 1919 Convention Relating to the Employment of Women, in McDougal et al (1967), op. cit., pp. 229-31.

6. On the meanings of these terms see Vandevelde (1988), op. cit.

7. See Article 32 of the Laws of Treaties in Shabatai (1989), op. cit., p. 458.

8. See, Blix, Hans, and Emerson, Jirina (1973), *The Treaty Makers' Handbook*, Oceana Publications, Inc., New York, pp. 270-1. For the English text of the Turkish-Jordanian treaty see, *United Nations Treaty Series* (1948), 'Treaty of Friendship between Turkey and the Hashemite Kingdom of Transjordan. Signed at Ankara, on 11 January 1947', vol. 14, pp. 55-7.

9. For the text of these treaties see Zafar Imam (1983), pp. 107-178.

10. One example is Cusimano, Joseph (1992), 'An Analysis of the Iran-Iraq Bilateral Border Treaties', *Case Western Reserve Journal of International Law*, vol. 24, no. 1, pp. 89-113; also see, Arndt, Clause (1980), 'Legal Problems of the German Eastern Treaties', *American Journal of International Law*, vol. 74, No. 1, p. 131.

11. See Russia's declaration of sovereignty in *Vedomosti S"ezda Narodnykh Deputatov RSFSR i Verkhovnogo Soveta RSFSR* (June 14, 1990), 'Deklaratsia: O gosudarstvennom suverenitete Rossiiskoi Sovetskoi Federativnoi Sotsialisticheskoi Respubliki', pp. 44-6.

12. 'Constitutive' recognition helps a state become sovereign and independent whereas 'declaratory' recognition simply offers recognition to an already sovereign and independent state under international law. See Brierly, James (1963), *The Law of Nations: An Introduction to the International Law of Peace*, sixth ed., Clarendon Press, Oxford, pp. 137-40.

13. For the text of the treaty see, *United Nations Treaty Series* (1947), 'Treaty of Alliance between His Majesty in Respect of the United Kingdom and his Highness the Amir of Transjordan. Signed at London, on 22 March, 1946', vol. 6, pp. 144-50.

14. See Article 3 of the Israeli-Jordanian Peace Treaty in *The New York Times* (October 27, 1994), p. A7.

15. On the issue of leaving clauses vague or very general see Bilder (1981), pp. 37-40; also see McDougal, Lasswell, and Miller (1967).

16. *Rossiiskaya gazeta* (April 12, 1991), 'Srokom na piat' let'', p. 1.

17. Kazakhstan, Ukraine, and Uzbekistan are selling uranium on the world market. The Russians have labelled this 'inept' competition with Russia which drives down the price of Russia's uranium. See Sosnov, Arkady (1994), 'Who Needs Russian Uranium?', *Moscow News* (September 23-9), no. 38, p. 7.

18. The Russians have long considered the Estonians stern negotiators. See Averchev, Vladimir (1994), 'The US Senate Resolution Will Only Hinder Negotiations', *Moscow News*, July 22-28, no. 29, pp. 1, 4.

19. For the text of the agreement see *Ekho Litvy* (August 1, 1991), 'Soglashenie mezhdu Litovskoi Respublikoi i Rossiiskoi Sovetskoi Federativnoi Sotsialisticheskoi Respublikoi o sotrudnichestve v ekonomicheskom i sotsial'no-kulturnom razvitii Kaliningradskoi oblasti RSFSR', pp. 1, 4.

8 Conclusion

Introduction

During the civil war which began soon after the October revolution in 1917, the Caucasian countries were independent for a very short period. They could form an alliance with the white general Anton Denikin's Volunteer Army. But such an alliance was ruled out because of Denikin's insistence that Russia's pre-war boundaries must be restored which would effectively end the Caucasian countries' independence. Just because Denikin was hostile to the Bolsheviks did not mean that he would accept Russia's loss of territory (Goldenberg, 1994, pp. 35-36). The similarity between Denikin's orientation and the Russian government's attitudes towards the former Soviet republics is too clear to be overlooked. It is true that Yeltsin and his associates fostered intense dislike for the hard-line communists and the indecisive, contradictory, reform steps taken by Gorbachev, but that did not necessarily mean that these parties would differ significantly when Russian interests were concerned regarding these peripheral countries.

This study has examined the RSFSR government's cooperation with the Soviet republics during the period June 1990-August 1991. I adopted a systemic approach to gain insight into the nature of the cooperation process and the character of the emerging state, Russia. The objective was to separate a series of interconnected activities of a major actor on the Soviet scene at an important but chaotic period in Soviet history and dissect them using prevalent research approaches and theoretical frameworks. In shedding light on the disintegration of the Soviet Union, I also hoped to illuminate

126 *Inter-republican cooperation*

Russia's actions in the post-Soviet space.

In this concluding chapter, I look at the whole cooperation process between Russia and the other republics in light of the findings in the previous chapters. The theoretical and practical implications of the findings are also discussed.

Russia's cooperation in terms of the actions

First I insulated the transactions which took place between Russia and its partners in the form of events data. This was done with the purpose to look at the nature of the actual interactions and the pattern they formed. Such patterns were to indicate whether it was an unidimensional process, a sudden initiative to impose control on the political and economic environment, or a well thought out policy to achieve certain broad goals.

The collected data show that numerous interactions took place in this short period under study. A large number of treaties were signed, important visits took place, and meetings were held to discuss significant issues of bilateral relations. Yeltsin himself visited Estonia, Kazakhstan, Kyrgyzstan, Latvia, and Ukraine. There were plans that he would visit Lithuania but the visit never took place. Prime Minister Silaev, and deputy speaker of the parliament, Ruslan Khasbulatov as well as the chair of the parliamentary committee on Inter-republican Relations and Regional Politics, Alexander Granberg were also involved in conducting inter-republican cooperation.

These varied set of interactions shows that the RSFSR conducted not a unidimensional but a multifaceted cooperation process. It was not simply economic cooperation to retain the previous Soviet period ties between Russia and the republics but a process which aimed at the formal-legal sovereignty of the republics in the context of a unified market economy and a territory safeguarded by a single defence system.

The third chapter demonstrates that different sets of interactions served separate aims -- some of them began the cooperation process by signalling Russia's intent, some circumscribed the central government's authority, some displayed the Russian government's support for the republican governments. A part of these aggregate interactions affirmed Russia's willingness to accept the republics as sovereign entities, another portion of the actions were used to lock the republics in an intimate relation with Russia. The first type were the statements Russian leaders made, their visits to republics that were laden with symbolic importance, and joint declarations and communiques which are not binding under international law. The second type were primarily the basic treaties on inter-state relations and some agreements signed after signing the treaties on inter-state relations.

The RSFSR leaders' valuable symbolic support for the republics' demands and their willingness to recognize them as sovereign states undercut the leadership of Gorbachev. These actions suggested to the domestic audience and foreign observers that Russian officials were much more lenient than the Gorbachev government. The central government adamantly refused to yield to republican demands for sovereignty and harshly treated those republics which dared to declare sovereignty as Lithuania did in March 1990 and quickly found itself under an economic blockade imposed by the central government. Thus Russian lenience in contradistinction to the central leadership's obduracy put Russia in a favourable position vis a vis the central government in relation to the republican leaders. This was especially true as regards the governments of the Baltic republics, the two Caucasian republics of Armenia and Georgia, the two Slavic republics of Belarus and Ukraine, Moldova, and two Central Asian republics of Kazakhstan and Kyrgyzstan.[1] Thus a majority of the republics found what Russia said attractive and was willing to try out relations with Russia. Russia was boosted as the leader in the centre-periphery debate which inevitably eroded Gorbachev's ability to recreate the Union as a more flexible structure of a federative state.

On the other hand, the elaborate treaties with the misleading titles of 'Treaties on the Bases of Inter-State Relations' which were signed with a majority of the republics (the one with Armenia was drafted) are the actions which were used to tie up the republics. As analysed in chapter seven, these treaties safeguarded the interests of a disintegrating empire by using different treaty making tactics. The preambles of the treaties and their border provisions have been used to underscore that Russia was not accepting them as independent states but sovereign ones. Only the Baltic republics were allowed the rights to be independent states. The dispute resolution provisions of the treaties also underlined this orientation of Russia.

It was the treaties and agreements which delineated the nature of future political and economic relations between Russia and the treaty signing republics. Excepting the Baltic republics and Ukraine all the republics promised to work to create a renewed union. Although the terminology used in the three Baltic treaties was somewhat different from those in the non-Baltic treaties, all the republics pledged to retain and further develop extremely close economic relations. Excepting Lithuania which by and large got the most favourable treatment in the treaty making exercise, all the republics promised to develop a Eurasian and all European common market. They would cooperate at different levels of economic activities, government, enterprise, individual.

More constricting than the pledges on economic ties were the foreign policy commitments. Belarus, Kazakhstan, Kyrgyzstan, and Ukraine all were going to coordinate foreign policy actions with Russia. They would also be in a collective security system. Although the Baltic treaties were more flexible in wording they were also to coordinate foreign policy actions with Russia. It is true that the Baltic republics were not going to be part of the collective security system, but their future behaviour in terms of joining alliances were severely restricted by requiring them to either sign treaties on foreign policy cooperation or by not allowing them to join any other collective security system. Thus the republics were to be economically and politically linked with Russia.

The cooperative actions themselves support the assumptions in the two main theses that the Russian Republic conducted its cooperation policy with an eye to undercut the Gorbachev government and reorganize its relations with the republics so Russian interests would be carefully safeguarded. Its attempts, as demonstrated in the provisions of the treaties, to keep the republics in a tight security and economic embrace closely resemble attempts by the governments of collapsing empires to salvage imperial interests.

The Estonian leaders advised the Russian leaders to free themselves from their ties to the old empire and envisage Russia's future as that of just another republic hitherto oppressed by the communist Union government. The Russian government did declare Russia was just another republic and had been exploited by the communists who subscribed to an alien ideology. It tried to identify with the other republics through symbolic acts of solidarity and support. But its support for the republics' demand for sovereignty was more rhetorical than real. It went further than the Gorbachev government but not much further. When the question of legal reconstruction of relations came Russia's position was not that different from that of the Gorbachev government.

The analysis of the cooperative interactions themselves has voided one of the assumptions from which the book emanated. That assumption was Russia was ready to accept the republics as independent states under international law. It has been implicit although never stated clearly that the Russian government was so flexible that it was willing to accept the republics as independent states. The rhetoric of the Russian leaders contributed to the formation of such an assumption. Clearly, the Russian Republic, as stipulated in the treaties, was not forthcoming enough to accept the non-Baltic republics as independent.

Another implicit assumption of the study was Russia did not differentiate among republics. As the third thesis stipulates, it wanted to salvage Russian interests by establishing equally close ties with the republics.

But in the treaties, the main instrument used to link the republics, it differentiated between the Baltic and non-Baltic states. The Russian leaders accepted only the Baltic republics as independent states. This happened because the Baltic republics were independent till 1939, the West never accepted their annexation, and the republics had tough negotiation tactics. It was important for Yeltsin to strengthen his support among the Western governments, particularly the United States. The Bush administration did not want to destabilize the Gorbachev government by supporting republican leaders, but it softened enough in this regard to warn Yeltsin about impending coup attempts in Spring 1991. It should also be mentioned that the US government shared extensively intelligence reports with the Russian government during the August 1991 coup. Yeltsin did gain credibility among Western governments, his policy towards the Baltic republics, no doubt, contributed to this.

Russia's cooperation through elite utterances

The key components in any cooperation process are the different types of cooperative actions and interactions. That was the case with Russia. These interactions did not take place in a conceptual vacuum. They were accompanied by well articulated statements of the Russian decision makers as to what those interactions were, why Russia engaged in those, what the Russian government expected them to lead to. These statements were analysed in chapter six to put the cooperative actions themselves into perspective.

By carefully hammering on the themes of an alternative union which would be primarily an economic union the Russian government underlined that it did not want the republics to become independent states and then become a loose economic union like the European Community. It declared time and again that its treaties with the republics were the instruments with which a different kind of union was being forged from below. Prominent Russian leaders stressed that they left the central government and came to the Russian government because they thought Russia would rebuild the union. Affirmation of republican sovereignty remained a minor theme in their statements.

Their view of the union's future never included the republics as independent states. The Soviet Union was to remain one economic space with one monetary system. This economic space was simply to be a market economy rather than retain social-democratic characteristics as Gorbachev would have it. After the Union legislature rejected the Shatalin-Yavlinsky

Plan, Russia insisted on reform at the union level denying that it should and could do it alone. It was only reluctantly that the Russian Prime Minister later came up with a reform plan for Russia. Some of the ministers, for instance the finance minister, were clearly thinking about a decentralized federation in place of the Soviet Union.

Russian politicians frequently compared what Russia was doing with what would come of the super centralized structure of the Soviet state thus presenting its offer as an infinitely better deal. In their words it was Russia and its view of relations among the republics exemplified by its cooperation with them which could stabilize the situation. Elite pronouncements also captured some fear of the degenerating chaos which needed to be controlled through cooperation with the republics rather than using coercion as the Union government was doing.

When I began research for the analysis, I did not expect the theme of the Union to be so prominent. I believed I would find Russian decision makers to be emphasizing the sovereignty of the republics more.

The republics and Russia's cooperation

The manner in which the theses are articulated, the theoretical discussion is set forth, and the events data analysis is framed prompts one to assume that the republics were mere pawns in a fierce struggle between two titanic actors, the central government and Russia. The two chapters constituting the case study demonstrate that the nature of the cooperation process was at least partially determined by the demands and skills of the republics themselves.

Lithuania was most aggressive about its own agenda and wooed Russia with an intensity and persistence not found in Russia's interaction with any other republic. Lithuanian nationalist leaders, led by Vytautas Landsbergis, decided to identify Lithuania with Russia as closely as possible. They offered moral support to the Russian government and the democratic supporters of the Russian government, they provided the striking coal miners -- an important support base of the Russian government -- with material assistance. At a grassroots level, they tried to win the hearts of the ordinary Russians. They contributed much to achieving Russia's purpose to enfeeble the central government by accepting Russia as the proper partner in negotiations for Lithuania's future. This ardent courtship of Russia by Lithuania definitely determined the number of interactions that took place between Lithuania and Russia as well as -- to some degree -- the extent of Russia's support.

All the other republics, including the other two Baltic republics, did not fling themselves into the RSFSR's embrace as readily as did Lithuania. Estonia and Latvia did not want to completely write off the centre and thus arouse its wrath. They also did not feel Russia could supply their needs because it had not yet established enough control over the enterprises and resources on its own territory. To minimize their risks, they negotiated with the centre on economic matters and also negotiated with the RSFSR on the Treaty on the Bases of Inter-State Relations.

The strength of the Ukrainian nationalist movement made Ukraine more eager to team up with Russia. Ukraine was ambivalent about even signing the new Union Treaty that Russia was crucial in bringing about. Such a centrifugal orientation of Ukraine resulted in its signing more than one agreement with Russia and playing an important role on articulating the alternative vision for the Union in early 1991. Because of its cultural and ethnic linkages with Russia, Belarus seemed incapable of resisting Russian overtures and gravitated to the direction that Russia was moving especially after Shushkevich became leader of the parliament. The Moldovan nationalist movement was strong and the Moldovan government welcomed the Russian flexibility towards the republics. Moldova was one of the first republics to sign a major treaty with the RSFSR.

Among the Caucasian republics, Armenia and Georgia were led by leaders who strongly desired independence and were disillusioned with the central government. In Georgia's case, Zviad Gamsakhurdia, a former dissident, was the president of the republic. He was opposed to any kind of central government believing the republics as sovereign states could realize their own potential and develop relations among themselves without the mediation of a central government. Naturally, Russian lenience appealed to Gamsakhurdia's Georgia. Armenia, not unlike Lithuania, seemed to seize upon the opportunity to cooperate with a Russia that was hostile to the Union government. President Levon Ter-Petrosyan of Armenia sometimes initiated interactions with Russia and tried to offer Armenia as an ally. His government sought support from Russia in the territorial dispute with Azerbaijan. By contrast, Azerbaijan was under the leadership of Ayaz Mutalibov, a staunch, self-proclaimed pro-Moscow leader of the Soviet period as well as the post-Soviet period. It was predictable that Azerbaijan was cautious about going against the central government.

The Central Asian republics were the real dependent, periphery of the Soviet Union. The governments of these republics were led by politicians such as Nursultan Nazarbaev, Islam Karimov, and Rahman Nabyev who were not contemplating independence from the Soviet Union given their inability to survive on their own as largely self-sufficient economies. The Kazakh leader, Nazarbayev, endowed with the stature of a major political figure on the Union level, the quintessential moderate as he was, did not envisage the break-up of the Soviet Union. He wanted economic ties to remain and probably felt working with the Russian government would bear fruits in that regard. Russia of course tried to attract Nazarbayev to strengthen its own position. Kyrgyzstan was the Central Asian republic which, with Ashkar Akayev at the helm, was most eager to cooperate with Russia. Akayev was and is very different from the leaders of the other Central Asian republics. He was an intellectual reformer rather than a party official who came to power passing through the party hierarchy. This certainly influenced his government's decision to ally with the Russian leaders. Kyrgyzstan was also the first Central Asian republic to declare independence after the August 1991 coup.

It was somewhat different for the other three Muslim republics, Tajikistan, Turkmenistan, and Uzbekistan. No interaction has been recorded between Russia and Tajikistan. Tajikistan was too dependent on the Soviet economy with its cotton based economy and the republic's government being controlled by its pro-Moscow communist leaders. Although the Tajik polity was pulled into two directions, the democratic-Islamic opposition and the Tajik Communist Party, the communists retained a firm grip on power. Tajikistan did not display any interest to experiment with the Russian offer. This was more or less the case with Turkmenistan. The Uzbek case has been slightly different. Commentators at one point were murmuring that Russia had lost Uzbekistan to the centre with Russia protesting that it was conducting talks with the Uzbek government. There was hardly any interaction with Uzbekistan in 1990. But the situation changed in 1991 with Uzbekistan participating in multi-lateral actions to articulate the idea of an alternative Union.

It would be wrong to posit that the Central Asian republics, since they did not avidly respond to the Russian call for cooperation, did not seek independence. Indeed Uzbekistan declared sovereignty only about three months after Lithuania did (Pravda Vostoka, June 22, 1990, p. 1). In the post-Soviet period, Islam Karimov, the Uzbek President, along with Leonid Kravchuk of Ukraine, has been a vehement opponent of a strong union among the former Soviet republics.[2] Turkmenistan did its part to scuttle the plan for an economic union. These republics simply were forced to be more cautious and probably did not feel replacing the dominance of the communist union government with dominance by a non-communist Russia was a better bargain.

Conclusion 133

Theoretical implication

This study has drawn upon two theoretical orientations, i.e., elite conflict and dissolution of empires. It was presumed that the leading members of the Russian government were a segment of the communist elite which had been governing the USSR. This elite had stronger reformist aptitude than the central government under Gorbachev. An elite conflict began when Yeltsin with his close associates broke away from the central leadership. As the reforms of the Gorbachev leadership faltered, more and more members of the old elite abandoned Gorbachev. They helped form a Russian Republican leadership which transformed Russia into a stronghold of reformist opposition. Russia's inter-republican cooperation was a manifestation of the elite conflict. It was waged to undermine Gorbachev and seriously weaken his ability to renew the Soviet state structure as a federative entity. This part of the argument was anchored in elite conflict theory.

The second part of the argument was grounded in the literature on disintegration of empires and emergence of independent states in their place. I argued that Russia's cooperation with the other republics should not be viewed as the cooperation of just another republic with the rest because Russia was not the same as any other republic by virtue of its status in the putative Soviet empire as its core. Accordingly, the fact that there was an elite conflict and the Russian elites were a rebellious group from the old elite did not necessarily mean that they would have a drastically different outlook towards the periphery. I articulated the thesis that through the cooperation process the Russian government was trying to manage the uncontrolled disintegration of the empire and safeguard the interests of an empire as any governing elite of an imperial state would.

The quantitative and non-quantitative information on the Russian elites together indicate that there was a serious elite conflict the initial phase of which resulted in Yeltsin's ouster from the Politburo. Before his important speech to the CC in October 1987, Yeltsin had given serious thoughts to splitting the CPSU. Later his long time protege, Oleg Lobov, almost became the leader of the Russian Communist Party when it was formed. The biographical data presented in Appendix A demonstrate that an overwhelming majority of the Russian ministers came from the old Soviet elite. When the Russian Prime Minister, Ivan Silaev, was proposing his cabinet to the Russian parliament there was some protest from the floor that the cabinet was being formed with the party elites. On various occasions the leaders of the Russian government commented that they had left the Union government believing they would be able to carry out reforms more effectively from Russia.

Elite conflicts can be at the roots of major political developments just as such conflicts themselves appear at times of significant socio-political developments. Large-scale conflicts can be instrumental in spelling the doom of gigantic states as it happened in the Soviet Union. Virulent elite conflicts have been characteristic more of non-democratic states than democratic ones. This is proved not only by the conflict that occurred in the Soviet Union but the current one going on in Mexico which some observers have labelled a civil war between the traditional and reformist elements of the PRI. The latest demonstration of the conflict has been the protest of the governing elites of the State of Tobasco against the national government's democratization pact with the opposition concluded in January 1995. Some authors have noted that the leaders of the Islamic movements in the North African and Middle Eastern countries had been integral parts of the nationalist elites who were fighting for independence against the colonial rulers (Salame, 1993). With the tide of democracy prevailing serious system-threatening elite conflicts will be less evident.

Did the elite conflict make any difference as regards the demands of the majority of the republics for independence? Did the republics gain more because of the elite conflict? The Yeltsin government wanted to manage the dissolution of the empire because it found the political situation too volatile. This has been a key assumption in the book. This does not necessarily mean that the republics were going to achieve independence quickly. An uncontrolled deterioration of the situation could lead to repression accompanied by violence because the genie of nationalism could not be put back into the bottle.

Seen from this perspective, the elite conflict definitely benefited the republics' aspiration for independence. Gorbachev's reform efforts resulted in cracks in the ruling elite. In the resultant competition Yeltsin offered a better deal to the republics to win them over to his side. The Chinese reform initiative has not experienced any such major elite conflicts because consensus on the nature of reforms has been maintained with much care.[3] As a consequence any rival elite group has not been around offering sovereignty to either Tibet or Xinjiang. Sovereignty is not equivalent to total independence but can become a basis for that if significant chaos engulfs the imperial state. In the post-Soviet period the Russian elites are much less forthcoming than they were in the Soviet period when the process of inter-republican cooperation was gaining momentum. In 1993 Georgia was willing to sign a broad-based treaty with the Russians but the Russians wanted stipulations dictating Georgian state structure. They demanded that Georgia must have a federal state structure (Mikadze, October 15, 1993, p. 4). This was a more stringent condition than any in the treaties studied in chapter seven in which Russia did not pressure any republic to accept provisions relating to the structure of the state.

The republics of the Soviet Union observed the Russian elites' willingness to accept them as sovereign states through legal documents; for them, the distance from sovereignty to independence was a short one to traverse when the opportunity came. That came after the coup when both the Soviet and Russian states were extremely weak. The republican leaders struck when the iron was hot -- so to speak.

But elite conflict is one dimension of the argument. Does the evidence support the argument that Russia was also trying to manage the uncontrolled dissolution of the empire? The idea seemed odd when the research for this analysis began because the Yeltsin leadership still captivated political observers with its allegiance to radical reforms and democratic values. This is why, as mentioned in chapter six, historian Dunlop was surprised that Yeltsin, with his solid democratic credentials, was supporting Gorbachev in maintaining the Union. But in light of the evidence presented in this study such behaviour could be explained, if not predicted. Many have recently noticed that Russia is appearing more and more like the Soviet Union.

While Russia showed its willingness to give the republics more than what Gorbachev would, it made clear that its goal was to reconstruct the Union as a more viable structure. Elite pronouncements to the effect that Russia's cooperative interaction was a means to recognize the republics as sovereign states was moderated by declarations that they were also constituting the bases for a better Union. Members of the Russian government did not envisage a future for Russia separate from the Union. Russia was to be the pivot around which the reform effort would move.

The treaties signed by the Russian Republic with the other republics were the main instruments for retaining disproportionately more influence over the republics that were being recognized as sovereign states. The republics committed themselves to creating an economic union, a political union, and a defence union with Russia. The Baltic treaties were a little different but they also stipulated extremely close linkages. The republics agreed to such strict conditions as not to do any damage to the Russian economy as well as let Russia defend the rights of the Russian minorities living on their territories.

The similarities between Russian efforts to keep intimate linkages with the republics and the efforts of past empires to limit their losses resulting from the independence of their former colonies are too strong to be ignored. Britain, Belgium, France all acted in similar fashions. Some Russian ministers even mentioned that the RSFSR was aiming at a commonwealth like the British Commonwealth.

The Russian actions resemble more those of the French when the French colonies in Africa opted for independence. France, under a charismatic leader, Charles de Gaulle, was in the process of pulling itself out from the chaotic fourth republic and trying to create a more stable fifth republic. The African countries like Gabon, Ivory Coast, Mali, Mauritania, Niger, Senegal, were demanding more autonomy. France offered to create a French community of states. The community did not work. The African states demanded full independence. France quickly agreed to give them independence but wanted to sign cooperation treaties which would establish close diplomatic, cultural, economic, and defence relations. Some states were allowed not to have defence relations just like the Baltic republics in their treaties with Russia. It is true that when the African countries became associate members of the European Community the French influence lessened somewhat but French cultural, economic, and military dominance over its former colonies is still undisputed.[4]

There are some differences. The geographic proximity between Russia and the republics makes Russia only more tenacious in its persistence to retain the republics in its grip. While France first tried multilateral ties and then abandoned them switching on to bilateral relations, Russia has been moving on both the fronts simultaneously. The ties sought by Russia are thus somewhat stronger.

The use of theories of elite conflict and imperial disintegration has indeed helped study the phenomenon, but this does not mean some strands of the coalition theory could not further enrich the study. There clearly were some coalition building and maintenance strategies being used. Russia signed and ratified the major treaties first with Belarus, Kazakhstan, and Ukraine. These were also the republics which interacted in early 1991 to come out with the model of an alternative Union. Russia, Ukraine, Kazakhstan, and Belarus were the republics working out this alternative idea. Coalitions are also maintained by avoiding controversial issues so unity against the common foe could be nurtured. This was done by Russia as well as the republics. For instance, Russia did not raise territorial claim over Crimea and Estonia kept silent about the Pechora district. Pechora was acknowledged as belonging to Estonia in the 1920 treaty signed between Estonia and Russia and recently Estonia has claimed the territory infuriating the Russian government.

Practical implications

This study has focused on Russian relations with the fourteen republics in a crucial period in the history of this region, making it useful in understanding Russia's behaviour and the process of development of the CIS in the post-Soviet setting. Past cooperation clearly impacts upon the potential for future cooperation. One of the tenets of coalition theory is that experience in coalition maintenance influences future coalition behaviour.

Whereas other republics, with the exception of Kazakhstan, have been skeptical about the CIS, Russia has relentlessly pursued the goal of making the CIS work even if that has to be done slowly and in numerous stages. Only the Baltic states have been allowed to exist outside the CIS as was clear from early on. Georgia and Azerbaijan have been made to heed Russia's wishes. In Georgia it happened through Gamsakhurdia's ouster and Edward Shevardnadze's coming to power and Russian aid to Abkhaz nationalists (Fuller, 1994, p. 105). In Azerbaijan, the popularly elected nationalist government of Abul Faz Elchibey was overthrown and the former Azerbaijan party chief Gaider Aliyev returned to power. Now that Aliyev is trying to look after Azerbaijani interests more, the ground for his replacement with much more pro-Moscow Ayaz Mutalibov is being prepared. Tajikistan has become a virtual protectorate of Russia. It must coordinate its financial and taxation policy with the Central Bank of Russia and its economic mechanisms must be brought into line with those of Russia (Shermatova, December 3, 1993, p. 4). In 1993, agreement was reached between Russia, Georgia, and the Central Asian states for the maintenance of Russian soldiers and military bases at their own expense. When Shevardnadze hesitated the Russian defence minister Pavel Grachev presented him with the following scenario: Russia would withdraw its troops from Georgia and Georgia could face nationalist rebellion on its own (Zhilin, September 10, 1993, p. 3). Turkmenistan must sell its oil under a quota assigned to it by Russia (Shermatova, September 30-October 6, 1994, p. 5).

Over the past three years the CIS had not been able to get off the ground (Olcott, 1994, p. 35). 1994 has been a better year for the CIS because a collective security agreement has been signed and a payment union has been agreed upon. The republics have been very wary about ending up in a union not significantly different from the Soviet Union. If the pre-coup cooperation process had not been a Russian effort to manage the break-up of the Soviet empire defining Russian interests so broadly, Russia could have become more of a trustworthy partner and the development of the CIS could have been smoother and more propitious. The experience of cooperation with Russia would have worked as a positive factor.

Notes

1. The Kazakh leader, Nursultan Nazarbaev, was a special case. He was on good terms both with the central government and Russia.

2. Karimov has described suggestions to delegate some republican powers to the central CIS structures as 'treachery ... and an attempt to reverse the course of history', quoted in Usmanov, Lerman (September 10, 1993), 'Will Islam Karimov become a Nobel Prize Winner?', *Moscow News*, no. 37, p. 5.

3. On elite unity in the Chinese reform project see Johnson, Juliet (1994), 'Should Russia Adopt the Chinese Model of Economic Reform', *Communist and Post-Communist Studies*, vol. 27, no. 1, pp. 59-75.

4. For the decolonization process in French Africa and the post-colonial relations between the former metropole and its colonies see, McNamara, Francis (1989), *France in Black Africa*, National Defence University, Washington D.C., especially chapters two and three. Also see Johnson, G.W. (1985), 'Conclusion: The Legacy of French Colonial Rule and Double Impact' in Johnson, G.W. (ed), *Double Impact: France and Africa in the Age of Imperialism*, Greenwood Press, Westport, Connecticut, pp. 379-390.

Appendix A
Occupational Backgrounds of RSFSR Ministers, 1990

The following is a list of RSFSR ministers' names, their current portfolios, their immediate past occupation, in that order.

1. Barannikov, V., RSFSR minister, Internal Affairs; RSFSR 1st deputy minister of Internal Affairs of General Matters.

2. Bulgak, V., RSFSR minister, Communications, Information Science and Space; member of Collegium, USSR Ministry of Communications.

3. Cheshinsky, L., RSFSR minister, Grain Products; RSFSR deputy minister, procurement, since 1983.

4. Dneprov, E., RSFSR minister, Education; director of an academic institute.

5. Feodorov, B., RSFSR minister, Finance; staff member of Economics Department of CC CPSU.

6. Feodorov, D., chair of RSFSR State Committee on Geology, Fuel, Energy Carriers and Mineral Resources; director, Lower Volga Research Institute of Geology Geophysics.

7. Feodorov, N., RSFSR minister, Justice; chair, Sub Committee for Social Legislation, USSR Supreme Soviet.

8. Fil'shin, G., RSFSR deputy premier; USSR deputy.

9. Gavrilov, I., chair, RSFSR State Committee on Ecology and Rational Use of Resources; worked as hydrologist.

10. Ivchenko, S., RSFSR minister, Social Security; past occupation unknown.

11. Kalinin, V., RSFSR minister, Health; past occupation unknown.

12. Khlystov, A., RSFSR minister, Trade; General Director, 'Mosinter' All Union Association, had worked as lieutenant colonel in the K.G.B.

13. Kisin, V., RSFSR minister, Industry; deputy chair, Sub commission on

Development of Industry, Power Engineering, Machine Building and Technology, USSR Supreme Soviet.

14. Kobets, K., RSFSR minister, Defence; deputy chief of staff, USSR Armed Forces.

15. Kozyrev, A., RSFSR minister, Foreign Affairs; head, International Organizations Department, USSR Foreign Ministry.

16. Kulik, G., RSFSR deputy premier; first deputy chair, RSFSR State Agro-Industrial Committee.

17. Maley, M., RSFSR deputy premier; past occupation unknown.

18. Malyshev, N., RSFSR deputy premier; rector, a Radio Engineering Institute in Taganrog.

19. Poltoranin, M., RSFSR minister, Information and Media; editor-in-chief of Moskovskaya Pravda.

20. Shubin, V., RSFSR minister, Forestry; general director, Cheliabinsk Timber Production and Procurement Association.

21. Silaev, I., RSFSR prime minister; deputy chair, USSR Council of Ministers.

22. Skokov, Yu., RSFSR deputy premier; chair, Board of Moscow's 'Kvantemp' Production Association.

23. Solomin, Yu., RSFSR minister, Culture; Actor.

24. Vozhakov, V., chair, State Committee for Material and Technical Support of Republic and Regional Programs; deputy chair, USSR State Committee for Material and Technical Supply.

25. Yaroshenko, V., RSFSR minister, Foreign Economic Relations; chair, Sub Committee on Tax Policy, USSR Supreme Soviet.

26. Yavlinsky, G., RSFSR deputy premier; head, General Department, State Commission on Economic Reform, USSR Council of Ministers.

27. Yefimov, V., RSFSR minister, Transportation; RSFSR minister, Motor Vehicle Transport.

*The biographical information given here and throughout the book have been collected from the following sources: *Current Digest of the Soviet Press, FBIS, Moscow News, New Times, Rossiiskaya gazeta,* Sakwa (1993). Complete citations will be provided on request.

Appendix B
Officials with Personal Links with Yeltsin, June 90-Aug. 91

1. G. Burbulis, Yeltsin associate, managed his presidential campaign, college lecturer from Sverdlovsk.

2. V. Iliushin, head of the Secretariat of RSFSR Supreme Soviet and aide to Yeltsin, party official from Sverdlovsk.

3. O. Lobov, Yeltsin associate, vice premier of RSFSR (July, 1991), party official from Sverdlovsk.

4. V. Makharadze, managed Yeltsin's presidential campaign, came from Sverdlovsk.

5. Yu. Petrov, head of presidential administration of RSFSR, party chief in Sverdlovsk.

6. V. Semenchenko, Yeltsin aide, started political career as an aide to the Sverdlovsk party first secretary Yeltsin.

7. S. Shakhray, worked in Yeltsin presidential campaign, deputy in the RSFSR Supreme Soviet, came from Sverdlovsk.

8. L. Sukhanov, Yeltsin aide, worked with Yeltsin in USSR State Construction Committee.

9. Ye. Tkachenko, RSFSR first deputy minister of Education, rector of the Sverdlovsk Engineering and Teacher Training Institute.

10. A. Tsaregorodtsev, head of the Secretariat of RSFSR vice president, from Sverdlovsk.

11. P. Voshchanov, Press Secretary to RSFSR President, had close relations with Yeltsin since 1985.

12. V. Vozhakov, chairman of RSFSR State Committee for Material and Technical Support of Republic and regional Programs. Worked in Sverdlovsk during Yeltsin's tenure.

Appendix C
Categorization of Interactions

Agreements: This category represents all the formal treaties between Russia and other republics plus the unwritten agreements, both bilateral and multilateral. An overwhelming majority of the agreements were written agreements.

Appeals: Multilateral and unilateral appeals made by Russia. These appeals aimed at helping the republics or intensifying inter-republican cooperation.

Communications: Any public letter, telegram, or telephone calls made by the Russian government to the republics or by the republics to the Russian government. Communications initiated by the republics are included here to get a more balanced picture.

Communiques: All communiques and protocols signed by Russia with another republic, both bilateral and multilateral.

Declarations: Multilateral and bilateral declarations signed by Russia. One such declaration was the one signed by Russia and the Baltic republics which provided for them to come to one another's aid if any of them was attacked.

Meetings: Meetings between the Russian government and the republican governments. Includes routine negotiation sessions. Meetings to discuss issues during visits are included in the category.

Statements: Statements made to support the positions taken by the republics. One statement counted per occasion although more than one were made sometimes. In many cases, only one was made.

Represent Interests: Speaking on behalf of the republics or representing the interests of the republics to the centre.

Speech: Speeches delivered to a republican audience, e.g., the republican parliament.

Visit: Visits made to another republic by high level Russian officials, for example the prime minister, ministers, or the chair of the parliament.

144 Inter-republican cooperation

Other: All interactions that occurred less than twice. One example is Russia's participation, along with other republics, in a seminar that passed a resolution supporting republican independence.

Appendix D
Categorization of Themes

Union creation themes: Cooperation will lead to the renewal of the Union, this is building the Union from below, this is consolidation of a uniform position of the republics which will be presented as the basis of the Union Treaty, this is the rebirth of the Union as an economic Union, this will lead to the birth of a community of nations and similar themes.

Linkage preservation themes: Cooperation in general will strengthen the horizontal linkages, a particular treaty will expand the horizontal linkages, this is not the breakup of the Union, rather its continuation, this treaty is signed to preserve the historical ties that developed over a long stretch of time, this will preserve the Union as an economic Union, and similar themes.

Future linkage themes: This agreement will lead to many more agreements on different aspects of relations, there will be different kinds of close future economic cooperation, the treaties are signed to establish all kinds of, e.g., political, cultural, economic, diplomatic, relations, this will lead to cultural ties, and other like themes.

Defence themes: The defence themes could be put in the second or the third categories but I have kept them separate because of their importance. This category includes any idea dealing with collective security or any other kind of defence arrangement.

Ethnic issue themes: This category includes thoughts about safeguarding the rights of the Russian speaking population in the other republics. These themes usually were expressed in the following manners: this treaty will ensure equal citizenship to the Russian speaking population in this republic, this is the legal and peaceful way of securing the rights of the Russian speaking population in the other republics and so on.

Uncertainty themes: Ideas that Russia was engaging in the cooperation process because of the uncertain and unstable condition of the country were arranged under this category. Such themes included the following: Russia was signing such treaties or conducting negotiations to stabilize the collapsing economy, to facilitate transition to the market economy through reform coordination, because the signing of the Union Treaty was not certain at all.

146 *Inter-republican cooperation*

Comparison themes: Reasons given for Russian cooperation which compared Russian activities to those of the centre, example, this is a departure from tradition, this is a more efficient way of solving problems.

Sovereignty themes: Affirmation of republican sovereignty. Ideas that inter-republican cooperation activities were carried out to give content to the republican declarations of sovereignty, that these actions were those of equal partners and so forth.

Identification themes: There were very few instances of such themes occurring. The few times that they occurred they did so in the following form: Russia was joining the defence of republican rights.

Neutral themes: These themes also occurred very infrequently. They are the ideas which did not fit in any of the above categories. They neither deal with linkages, nor with republican sovereignty. Their expression took different forms including the following: this treaty is the legal basis of the signing parties' relations, this treaty declares the rights of the republics. They were categorized as neutral because they do not give any indication of whether the relations that were being referred to were either imagined in the framework of the continuation of the current ties or establishment of future ties.

Bibliography

Primary Sources

Russian Language Sources

Newspapers:

Bakinskii Rabochii
Ekho Litvy
Izvestia
Kazakhstanskaya Pravda
Pravda Ukrainy
Pravda Vostoka
Rossiiskaya gazeta
Slovo Kyrgyzstana
Sovetskaya Belorussiya
Sovetskaya Estonia
Sovetskaya Kyrgyzia
Sovetskaya Latvia
Sovetskaya Moldova

Government Sources:

Sbornik mezhdunarodnykh dogovorov SSSR i Rossiiskoi Federatsii (1992), vol. 47, Moscow: Mezhdunarodnaya otnosheniya.

Vedomosti s"ezda Narodnykh Deputatov RSFSR i Verkhovnogo Soveta RSFSR,Moscow: Supreme Soviet of the RSFSR, 1990-1993 consulted.

English Language Sources

Current Digest of the Soviet Press
Foreign Broadcast Information Service (FBIS)

Secondary Sources

Armstrong, Arthur (1981), 'Strategic Underpinnings of the Legal Regime of Free Association: The Negotiations for the Future Political Status of Micronesia', *Brooklyn Journal of International Law*, vol. 7, no. 2, pp. 204-5.
Arndt, Clause (1980), 'Legal Problems of the German Eastern Treaties', *American Journal of International Law*, vol. 74, no. 1.
Averchev, Vladmir (July 22-28, 1994), 'The US Senate Resolution Will Only Hinder Negotiations', *Moscow News*, pp. 1, 4.
Bahry, Donna (1991), 'Republican Economic Reform', *Nationalities Papers*, 19, Spring.
Baran, Paul (1957), *The Political Economy of Growth*, Monthly Review Press, New York.
Bartnikas, Stanislav, and Krutakov, Leonid, (August 5-11, 1994), 'Back to Pre-Petrine Rus?', *Moscow News*, no. 31.
Ben-Ami, Shlomo (1990), 'The Crisis of The Dynastic Elite in Transition from Monarchy to Republic, 1929-1931' in Lannon, Francis, and Preston, Paul (eds), *Elites and Power in Twentieth Century Spain*, Clarendon Press, Oxford, pp. 71-90.
Betteleheim, Charles (1976), *Class Struggle in the USSR*, Monthly Review Press, New York.
Bialer, Seweryn (1989), 'The Yeltsin Affair: The Dilemma of the Soviet Left in Gorbachev's Revolution' in Bialer Seweryn (ed.), *Politics, Society, and Nationality Inside Gorbachev's Russia*, Westview Press, Boulder, pp. 91-120.
_____ (1986), *The Soviet Paradox: External Expansion, Internal Decline*, Knopf, New York.
Bilder, Richard (1981), *Managing the Risks of International Agreements*, The University of Wisconsin, Madison.
Blix, Hans, and Emerson, Jirina (eds) (1973), *The Treaty Makers' Handbook*, Oceana Publications, Inc., New York.
Breslauer, George (1984), 'Is there a Generation Gap in the Soviet Political

Establishment? Demand Articulation by RSFSR Provincial Party First Secretaries', *Soviet Studies*, vol. 36, no. 1.
Brierly, James (1963), *The Law of Nations: An Introduction to the International Law of Peace*, sixth ed., Clarendon Press, Oxford.
Broadbent, Jeffrey (October, 1989) 'Strategies and Structural Contradictions: Growth Coalition Politics in Japan', *American Sociological Review*, vol. 54.
Browne, Eric, and Gleiber, Dennis (1986), 'Cabinet Stability in the French Fourth Republic: The Ramadier Coalition Government of 1947' in Pridham, Geoffrey (ed.), *Coalition Behaviour in Theory and Practice*, Cambridge University Press, London.
Burton, Michael, Gunther, Richard, and Higley, John (1992), 'Introduction: Elite Transformation and Democratic Regimes' in Higley, John, and Gunther, Richard (eds), *Elites and Democratic Consolidation in Latin America and Southern Europe*, Cambridge University Press, Cambridge, pp. 1-37.
Butterfield, Jim (1990), 'State Response to Informal Groups', *Nationalities Papers*, vol. 18, no. 2.
Carrere d'Encausse, Helene (1993), *The End of the Soviet Empire: The Triumph of the Nations*, Basic Books, New York.
Chiesa Giulietto, and Douglas Northorp (1993), *Transition to Democracy: Political Change in the Soviet Union*, The University Press of New England, Hanover.
Cusimano, Joseph (1992), 'An Analysis of the Iran-Iraq Bilateral Border Treaties', *Case Western Reserve Journal of International Law*, vol. 24, no. 1, pp. 89-113.
Czaplinski, Wladislaw (1992), 'The Polish-German Treaties and the Changing Political Structure of Europe', *American Journal of International Law*, vol. 86, no. 1, pp. 163-173.
Darwin, John (1991), *The End of the British Empire: The Historical Debate*, Basil Blackwell Inc., London.
Dittmer, Lowell (1990), 'Patterns of Elite Strife and Succession in Chinese Politics', 123, pp. 405-430.
Eckstein, Harry (1975), 'Case Study and Theory in Political Science' in Greenstein, Fred, and Polsby, Nelson (eds), *Handbook of Political Science*, vol. 7, Addison-Wesley, Reading, Massachusetts.
Eklof, Ben (1989), *Soviet Briefing: Gorbachev and the Reform Period*, Westview Press, Boulder.
Fox, Jonathan (1994), 'The Difficult Transition from Clientelism to Citizenship: Lessons from Mexico', *World Politics*, vol. 46, no. 2, pp. 151-184.

Frost, Howard (1989), 'A Content Analysis of Recent Soviet Party-Military Relations', *American Journal of Political Science*, vol. 33, no. 1, pp. 91-136.

Fuller, Graham (1994), 'Russia and Central Asia: Federation or Faultline?' in Mandelbaum, Michael (ed.), *Central Asia and the World: Kazakstan, Uzbekistan, Tajikistan, Kyrgyzstan, and Turkmenistan*, Council on Foreign Relations Press, New York.

Ganyushkin, Vitaly (September, 1993), 'The Commonwealth of Independent States: Realities and Prospects', *New Times International*, no. 37. p. 3.

Galtung, Johan, Heiestad, Tore, and Ruge, Eric (1979), *On the Decline and Fall of Empires: The Roman Empire and Western Imperialism Compared*, The United Nations University, Japan.

Gibbs, David (1991), *The Political Economy of Third World Intervention: Mines, Money, and US Policy in the Congo Crisis*, University of Chicago Press, Chicago.

Gleason, Gregory (December, 1991), 'The Political Economy of Dependency under Socialism: The Asian Republics in the USSR,' *Studies in Comparative Communism*, no. 4.

Goldenberg, Suzanne (1994), *Pride of Small Nations: The Caucasus and Post-Soviet Disorder*, Zed Books Ltd., London.

Goodman, Nancy (1991), 'Poland Bilateral Investment Treaty -- A Reflection of United States Efforts to Shape the Economic Development of Eastern Europe', *Harvard International Law Journal*, vol. 32, no. 1, pp. 255-264.

Hanson, Philip (1992), *From Stagnation to Catastroika: Commentaries on the Soviet Economy, 1983-1991*, Praeger, New York.

Harasymiew, Bohdan (1984), *Political Elite Recruitment in the Soviet Union*, Macmillan Press, London.

Hazard, John (1992), 'State, Law and the National Question in the USSR' in Motyl, Alexander (ed.), *The Post-Soviet Nations: Perspectives on the Demise of the USSR*, Columbia University Press, New York.

Hough, Jerry (Fall, 1990), 'Gorbachev's Endgame', *World Policy Journal*, vol. 7.

Imam, Zafar (1983), *Towards a Model Relationship: A Study of Soviet Treaties with India and other Third World Countries*, ABC Publishing House, New Delhi.

Jahan, Rounaq (1972), *Pakistan: Failure in National Integration*, Columbia University Press, New York.

Johnson, Juliet (1994), 'Should Russia Adopt the Chinese Model of Economic Reform?', *Communist and Post-Communist Studies*, vol. 27,

no. 1, pp. 59-75.
Johnson, Wesley (1985), 'Conclusion: The Legacy of French Colonial Rule and Double Impact' in Johnson, Wesley (ed.), *Double Impact: France and Africa in the Age of Imperialism*, Greenwood Press, Westport, Connecticut, pp. 379-390.
Kagarlitsky, Boris (1990), *Farewell Perestroika: A Soviet Chronicle*, Verso, New York.
Karatnycky, Adrian (August 30, 1994), 'Russia's Nuclear Grasp', *The New York Times*, p. A13.
Kashis, I. (September 5, 1990), 'Spasaite dushi parliamentariev,' under Daidzhest pressa Litvy, *Ekho Litvy*, p. 3.
Kirkilas, G. (September 19, 1990), 'Nedelia', under Daidzhest pressa Litvy, *Ekho Litvy*, p. 3.
Krippendorf, Klaus (1980), *Content Analysis: An Introduction to its Methodology*, Sage Publications, Beverly Hills.
Kux, Stephen (1990), *Soviet Federalism: A Comparative Perspective*, The Institute for East-West Security Studies, New York.
Lachman, Richard (1990), 'Class Formation Without Class Struggle: An Elite Conflict Theory of the Transition to Capitalism', *American Sociological Review*, vol. 55, no. 3, pp. 398-415.
_____ (1989), 'Elite Conflict and State Formation in the 16th and 17th Century England and France', *American Sociological Review*, vol. 54, no. 2, pp. 141-162.
Lapidus, Gail, Zaslavsky, Victor, and Goldman, Philip (1992), 'Introduction: Soviet Federalism -- Its Origins, Evolution, and Demise' in Lapidus, Gail, Zaslavsky, Victor, and Goldman, Philip (eds), *From Union to Commonwealth: Nationalism and Separatism in the Soviet Republics*, Cambridge University Press, Cambridge.
Laver, Michael, and Higgins, Michael (1986), 'Coalition or Fianna Fail?' in Pridham, Geoffrey (ed.), *Coalitional Behaviour in Theory and Practice*, Cambridge University Press, London, pp. 171-197.
Lenin, Vladimir (1926), 'Imperialism: The Last Stage of Capitalism' in Vladimir Lenin, *Imperialism; State and Revolution*, Vanguard Press, New York.
Levitsky, Leonid (August 6, 1990), 'Cherez baltiskoe rinok k rinku vsekh respublik' *Izvestia*, p. 2.
Liao, Kuang-Sheng (1984), *Antiforeignism and Modernization in China, 1860-1980: Linkage between Domestic Politics and Foreign Policy*, Chinese University Press, Hong Kong.
Malcolm, Neil (1988), 'Foreign Affairs Specialists and Decision Makers' in Lane, David (ed.), *Elites and Political Power in the USSR*, Edward

Elgar Publishing Ltd., Aldershot, pp. 205-244.
Malek, Mohammad (December, 1989), 'Elite Factionalism in the Post Revolutionary Iran', *Journal of Contemporary Asia*, vol. 4.
McDougal, Myres, Lasswell, Harold, and Miller, James (1967), *The Interpretation of Agreements and World Public Order: Principles of Content and Procedures*, Yale University Press, New Haven.
McNamara, Francis (1989), *France in Black Africa*, National Defence University, Washington D.C.
Migranian, A. (September 20, 1990), 'Soyuz ne rushimy: O perspectivakh Sovetskoi Gasudarstvennosti', *Izvestia*, p. 3.
Mikadze, Akaky (October 15-21, 1993), 'CIS Worse than Slavery?', *Moscow News*, no. 42, p. 4.
Mikhalskaya, T., and Orlov, V. (July 30-August 5, 1993), 'The President's Team: The First Circle', *Moscow News*, no. 31, p. 6.
Moltz, James (1993), 'Divergent Learning and the Failed Politics of Soviet Economic Reform', *World Politics*, vol. 45, pp. 301-326.
Motyl, Alexander (1991), 'Empire or Stability? The Case for Soviet Dissolution', *World Policy Journal*, vol. 8, no. 3.
Nederveen-Pieterse, Jan (1990), *Empire and Emancipation: Power and Liberation on a World Scale*, Pluto Press, London.
Nozari, Fairborz (1971), *Unequal Treaties in International Law*, S-Byran Sundt & Co., Stockholm.
Olcott, Martha (1994), 'Ceremony and Substance: The Illusion of Unity in Central Asia' in Mandelbaum, Michael (ed.), *Central Asia and the World: Kazakhstan, Uzbekistan, Tajikistan, Kyrgyzstan, and Turkmenistan*, Council on Foreign Relations Press, New York.
Orlov, Vladimir (June 17-23, 1994), 'Does Nuclear Ukraine Have a Future', *Moscow News*, no. 24, p. 4.
Osherov, R. (March 19, 1991), 'Demokrati vsekh respublik soedinaetes', *Ekho Litvy*, p. 2.
Otto, Robert (1990), 'Review Essay: Contemporary Russian Nationalism', *Problems of Communism*, vol. 39, no. 6.
Perez-Lopez, Jorge (1979), *Cuban International Relations: A Bilateral Agreements Perspective* (Northwestern Pennsylvania Institute for Latin American Studies, Erie Pennsylvania).
Popov, Gavril (1992), 'Avgust Devianosta Pervava', *Izvestia*, August 25-27.
Pridham, Geoffrey (1986), 'An Inductive Theoretical Framework for Coalitional Behaviour: Political Parties in Multi-Dimensional Perspective in Western Europe' in Pridham, Geoffrey (ed.), *Coalitional Behaviour in Theory and Practice*, Cambridge University Press, London, pp. 1-31.

Putnam, Robert (1976), *The Comparative Study of Political Elites*, Prentice Hall, Inc., Inglewood Cliffs.
Rahr, Alexander (1992), 'The Top Leadership: From Soviet Elite to Republican Leadership' in Lane, David (ed.), *Russia in Flux: The Political and Social Consequences of Reform*, Edward Elgar Publishing Ltd., Aldershot.
_____ (1990), *A Biographical Directory of 100 Leading Soviet Officials*, Westview Press, Boulder.
Reddaway, Peter (November, 7, 1991), 'The End of Empire', *New York Review of Books*, pp. 53-59.
Rigby, T.H. (1990), *Political Elites in the USSR: Central Leaders and Local Cadres from Lenin to Gorbachev*, Edward Elgar Publishing Ltd., Aldershot.
Robinson, Neil (July, 1992), 'Gorbachev and the Place of the Party in the Soviet Reform, 1985-'91', *Soviet Studies*, vol. 44, no. 3, pp. 423-444.
Roeder, Philip (1993), *Red Sunset: The Failure of Soviet Politics*, Princeton University Press, Princeton.
Rutland, Peter (March, 1991), 'The Search for Stability: Ideology, Discipline, and Cohesion of the Soviet Elite', *Studies in Comparative Communism*, no. 1.
Rywkin, Michael (1990), *Moscow's Muslim Challenge: Soviet Central Asia*, E. Sharp, New York.
Salame, Ghassan (1993), 'Islam and the West', *Foreign Policy*, no. 90, pp. 22-37.
Seliverstov, Vyacheslav (1991), Inter-republican Economic Interactions in the Soviet Union' in McAuley, Alastair (ed.), *Soviet Federalism: Nationalism and Economic Decentralization*, Leicester University Press, Leicester, pp. 111-127.
Senn, Alfred (1990), *Lithuania Awakening*, University of California Press, Berkeley.
Shabatai, Rosenne (1989), *Developments in the Law of Treaties, 1945-1986*, Cambridge University Press, Cambridge.
Sheinberg, M. (February 2, 1991), 'Nado stroit' novoe gosudarstvo', *Ekho Litvy*, p. 2.
Shermatova, Sanobar (October 28-November 3, 1994), 'Leaders Try to Renew the CIS', *Moscow News*, no. 43, p. 2.
_____ (September 30-October 6, 1994), 'Turkmenistan Considers Appointing a Shah', *Moscow News*, no. 39, p. 5.
_____ (December 3, 1993), 'Tajikistan Places Itself under the Protectorate of Russia', *Moscow News*, no. 49, p. 4.
Shevtsova, L. (September 17, 1990), 'Krizis vlasti: Pochemu on voznik i kak

iz nego vyiti', *Izvestia*.
Shinobu, Takashi (December, 1987), 'China's Bilateral Treaties, 1973-'82: A Quantitative Study', *International Studies Quarterly*, vol. 31, pp. 439-456.
Shved, V. (November 22, 1990), 'Mui vse plivem na odnom korable,' *Ekho Litvy*, p. 2.
Siaurusiavichius, A. (August 1, 1990), entry under Daidzhest pressa Litvy, *Ekho Litvy*, p. 3.
Smith, Raymond (1992), 'The Status of the Kaliningrad Oblast Under International Law', *Lituanus*, vol. 38, no. 1, pp. 7-52.
Solchanyk, Roman (1993), 'Russia, Ukraine, and the Imperial Legacy', *Post Soviet Affairs*, vol. 9, no. 4, pp. 337-365.
_____ (March, 1992), 'Ukraine, the (Former) Center, Russia, and "Russia"', *Studies in Comparative Communism*, pp. 31-45.
Sosnov, Arkady (September 23-29, 1994), 'Who Needs Russian Uranium?', *Moscow News*, no. 38, p. 7.
Stewart, Philip, Blough, Roger, and Warhola, James (1984), 'Soviet Regions and Economic Priorities: A Study in Politburo Perceptions', *Soviet Union*, vol. 11, part 1.
Suny, Ronald (1992), 'State, Civil Society, and Ethnic Cultural Consolidation in the USSR -- Roots of the National Question', in Lapidus, Gail, Zaslavsky, Victor, and Goldman, Philip, (eds), *From Union to Commonwealth: Nationalism and Separatism in the Soviet Republics*, Cambridge University Press, Cambridge.
Tammelo, Iimer (1967), *Treaty Interpretation and Practical Reason: Towards a General Theory of Legal Interpretation*, The Law Book Company Ltd., Sydney, Australia.
Tolz, Vera (1990), *The USSR's Emerging Multiparty System*, Praeger, Westport.
Toshchenko, Zh. (November 1, 1990), 'Tsentrism: Prognos na zavtra', *Izvestia*, p. 3.
Triska, Jan, and Slusser, Robert (1962), *The Theory, Law, and Policy of Soviet Treaties*, Stanford University Press, Stanford.
United Nations (1948), *United Nations Treaty Series*. vol. 14.
United Nations (1947), *United Nations Treaty Series*. vol. 6.
Urban, Michael (Spring, 1992), 'Boris Yeltsin, Democratic Russia, and the Campaign for the Russian Presidency', *Soviet Studies*, vol. 44, no. 2, pp. 87-207.
_____ (1988), 'Elite Stratification, and Mobility in a Soviet Republic' in Lane, David (ed.), *Elites and Political Power in the USSR*, Edward Elgar Publishing Ltd., Aldershot, pp. 127-163.

Usmanov, Lerman (September 10-16, 1993), 'Will Islam Karimov Become a Nobel Prize Winner?', *Moscow News*, No. 37, p. 5.
Vandevelde, Kenneth (1988), 'Treaty Interpretation from a Negotiator's Perspective', *Vanderbilt Journal of Transnational Law*, vol. 21, no. 2, pp. 281-311.
Wallerstein, Immanuel (1979), *The Capitalist World Economy: Essays*, Cambridge University Press, Cambridge.
Weber, Robert (1985), *Basic Content Analysis*, Sage Publications, Beverly Hills.
White, Stephen (July 1991), 'Rethinking the CPSU', *Soviet Studies*, vol. 43, no. 3.
Willerton, John (1992), *Patronage and Politics in the USSR*, Cambridge University Press, London.
_____ (1990), 'Reform, the Elite, and Soviet Center-Periphery Relations', *Soviet Union*, vol. 17, nos. 1-2.
Wishnevsky, Julia (1992), 'The Rise and Fall of "Democratic Russia"', *RFE/RL Research Report*, vol. 1, no. 22, pp. 23-27.
Wolfgang, Mommsen (1981), *Theories of Imperialism*, Weidenfeld and Nicolson, London.
Yeltsin, Boris (1990), *Against the Grain: An Autobiography*, Jonathan Cape, London.
Zaslavsky, Victor (1992), 'The Evolution of Separatism in Soviet Society under Gorbachev', in Lapidus, Gail, Zaslavsky, Victor, and Goldman, Philip (eds), *From Union To Commonwealth: Nationalism and Separatism in the Soviet Republics*, Cambridge University Press, Cambridge.
Zhilin, Alexander (September 10-16, 1993), 'Russian Military Presence in Georgia, Central Asia Reaffirmed', *Moscow News*, no. 37, p. 3.

Index

Abdullatipov, R. 32
Afanasyev, Yu. 52
Agreements: between Azerbaijan and Lithuania 48; Belarus and Ukraine 3;Lithuania and Tajikistan 48; Lithuania and Kyrgyzstan 48; Lithuania and Moldova 48; Lithuania and Armenia 47-8; Lithuania and Russia 46; Russia and Ukraine 36; economic 34, 98; cultural 103
Akayev, A. 99
Aliyev, G. 137
Alternative union 38-9, 90-1, 129
Armenia 3, 127, 131
audience bias 86
Azerbaijan 39, 131, 137
Azov sea 36

Baltic Council 58
Baltic republics 2, 4, 15, 41
Belarus 4, 127-8, 131, 136
Belgium 134
Bessmartnyk, A. 75
Bolshevik Revolution 52
Bonner, Y. 50

borders 112-13
Brazauskas, A. 79n
Britain 70, 135
British Commonwealth 17-20, 136
Bulgak, V. 14
Burbulis, G. 15

case study 23, 43-4
Central Committee (CPSU) 12, 14
centre-periphery relations 5
China 11
coalition: theories of 9
coal mine strike 61, 50
collective security 114-16
Commonwealth of Independent States (CIS) 4, 7, 82, 137
Communist elite 1-2
Communist Party: of the Soviet Union 2, 4, 6, 11, 12, 14, 52, 53, 59; of Russia 13
content analysis 22, 82-5

Darwin, J. 16-17
Declaration: of sovereignty 43, 110; of independence 113; of moratorium 64
Defence 94-5, 99, 114-16, 119

Democratic: alliance 19; Democratic Russia 14, 53, 58, 75, 81; Democratic Union 62n
Democratization: theories of 11
Denikin, A. 125
Dunlop, J. 82

economic blockade 44
economic union 38, 46, 91-2, 116-17, 120, 129
elite conflict: theory of 10; time of occurrence 11; in the Soviet Union 11, 133-4; in Gorbachev period 12
elite: circulation 10; convergence 10; settlement 10; theory 10; of Russia 10, 12, 20; of the Soviet Union 12-15, 24n
Elchibey, A. 137
Estonia 20, 126, 127, 136
Ethnic: conflict 95; issue 97; problems 36

Fil'shin, G. 13-14, 85-6
Foreign policy: coordination of 114-15, 119, 128
France: withdrawal from Africa 135

Gamsakhurdia, Z. 131
Gavrilov, A. 13
Georgia, 3, 127, 134, 137
Gorbachev, M.: and republican independence 15; and reform 5, 133-4; concession to Russia 56; and Russian government 127; and Yeltsin 59; Gorbachev and Yeltsin friction 12-13, 24n; Gorbachev government on Lithuania 76-7; on attacks on Lithuania 75; rapprochement with Russia 56, 71; western support for 70
Granberg, A. 46, 126

horizontal links 93-4

imperialism: theories of 16-18, 25n
International Court of Justice 107-8
Inter-Regional Group of Deputies 3-4
Iran 11
Ivanovo 53
Ivchenko, S. 13

Kalinin, V. 13
Kaliningrad 46, 120
Karimov, I. 131-2
Kazakhstan 4; 125-7, 135
Kempelman, M. 75
Khasbulatov, R. 16, 74, 86, 95, 126
Khrushchev, N. 11
Kiev 48
Kliamkin, E. 52
Kozyrev, A. 86, 95
Kravchuk, L. 99, 132
Kulik, G. 14
Kuzmitskas, B. 55, 64, 68-9
Kyrgyzstan 98, 126, 127-8

Lachman, R.11
Landsbergis, V.: and Gorbachev 66; on Soviet Union 66, 72, 73; and negotiations with Soviet Union 67, 68-9; and Russia 65, 69, 70-1; and Yeltsin 49
Latvia, 20, 126; Yeltsin's visit to 32;
Laws of treaties 106
Lithuania: and Russian democrats 50; gestures to Russia 49; intellectuals 70; January 91 attacks 45, 54-5, 73, 74; legislators and Soviet Union 66; Lithuanian-Russian relations 44-7, 50; Lithuania and the Soviet army 20, 77; media 70; Yeltsin's letter to the people of Lithuania 45-6
Lobov, O. 13, 15, 133

Maley, M. 13
Memorial 54
Minority: rights of 96, 103n, 113-14;

118
Moldova 126, 130
Moscow 72, 76, City Soviet 3; Party Committee 13;
Moteika, K. 64-5, 66
Multinational states 16
Multilateral conventions 108
Mutalibov, A. 130, 137

Nabyev, R. 130
Nagarno Karabakh 40
Nazarbaev, N. 131, 138n
Novichkov, V. 85

October, 1987 plenum 13
Ozolas, R. 57, 72

Patron-client politics: in Russia 14-15; theory 10
Pechora 136
Perestroika 12, 25, 54
People's diplomacy 50
Politburo (CPSU) 12
Poltoranin, M. 13, 74
Popov, G. 52, 57
Popular Fronts: Belarus Popular Front 2; Lithuanian Popular Front 2; Moscow Popular Front 2;
Protocol: signed by Estonia, Latvia and Russia 34-5; Georgia and Russia 36; recognizing Lithuania 45;
Prunskiene, K.: declaration with Landsbergis 73; on Landsbergis 68; on Soviet Union 64-5, 72; on Russia 72; on negotiations with Soviet Union 67, 71; telegram to Ryzhkov and Masliukov 72

rank ordering 99
Recognition: of republics as sovereign states 29-30, 33, 112, 121; kinds of 123n
regional cooperation: 9

Rodionov, V. 85
Russian: Russian Council of Ministers 13-14; Russian Democrats 49, 52-6, 59; Russian government 60; Russian heritage 6; Russian presidency 19, 26n, 53; Russian soldiers 36, 37 Russians 2; Russians and the Soviet Union 6, support for republics 127
Ryzhkov, N. 64, 67-8

Sajudis 49, 50, 55
Saudargas, A. 64-5, 66, 68, 75
Shakhray, S.15
Shchit 54
Shatalin-Yavlinsky Plan 91
Shelov-Kovedyaev, F. 95
Shevardnadze, E. 72, 137
Silaev, I.: and economic agreements 85; background of 13-14; letters to Latvia and Lithuania 31; on cooperation 98; proposes treaty to Azerbaijan 32; supporting Lithuania 58; supports republics 37
Skokov, Yu. 14
Sobchak, A. 52, 62n
South Ossetia 36
Solomin, Yu.13
Soviet Union: agreement with Russia 74; as an empire 8n, 16; breakup of 6, 127, 135; Russia's status in 2, 6; dictatorship 57, 74; Russian leaders on 96; treaties 107; treaty signing practice of 105;
Sukhanov, L. 15
Supreme Soviet: of Russia 3, 50, 58, 74; of the Soviet Union 57, 75
Stankevichius, Ch. 64-6
Sverdlovsk 12, 14-15, 53
Spain 11
Tajikistan 132, 137
Tallin conferences 38
Ter-Petrosyan, L. 40, 131-2

Travkin, N. 32
Treaty: between Armenia and Russia 33; Belarus and Russia 95; Estonia and Russia 33; Kazakhstan and Russia 33; Kyrgyzstan and Russia 33; Latvia and Russia 33; Lithuania and Russia 33, 45; Moldova and Russia 33; Russia and Turkmenistan 33; model 110; preambles 110-11; scope of treaties between Russia and the republics 109-10; subjective interpretation 107-8; teleological interpretation 108; textual interpretation 107; treaties on the bases of inter-state relations 33, 127, 131, 135
Turkmenistan 132

Ukraine 3-4, 126, 127-8, 131, 136
Union Treaty 2, 38, 48, 131
United States 68, 70
Uzbekistan 93, 132

Vagnarius, G. 51, 65, 67
Vilnius 48, 69, 72
Vozhakov, V. 14

West: on Lithuania 76, 79n
western observers 82

Yazov, D. 57, 74
Yefimov, V. 14